THE NON-FICTION BOOK

ENGLISH *& MEDIA* CENTRE

EMC KS3 ENGLISH SERIES

Acknowledgements

Written and edited by Sabrina Broadbent and Lucy Webster
with additional material by Barbara Bleiman and Jenny Grahame
Editorial Assistance: Guido Martini
Cover Blaise Thompson
Printed by Giunti Industrie Grafiche, Prato-Italy
Published by The English and Media Centre,
18 Compton Terrace, London N1 2UN
© 2001

Special thanks to Maggie O'Kane, Roger Clarke and Justine Picardie for agreeing to give their time to be interviewed.

Thanks to Penguin Books for extracts from *Letter to Daniel: Despatches from the Heart* by Fergal Keane and 'Side Effects' from *Pure Drivel* by Steve Martin. *The Guardian* and the authors for extracts from the following articles 'Soft Toys With Hard Centres' (Jack Schofield), 'Dead Man Walking' (Nancy Banks Smith). 'Desperate Bosnians Risk Minefield Deaths For US Army Rations' (Maggie O'Kane) and 'The Cruellest Choice' (editorial); Helge Rubinstein for an extract from *The Chocolate Book*; *The Telegraph* and Jim Muir for an extract from 'Five Die as Serbs'; Exploratorium for extracts from 'The Sweet Lure of Chocolate' (Jim Spadaccini); Vermillion for an extract from *Slim for Life* by Judith Wills; *The Independent* and authors for 'Dirty Dogs campaign: Foul Facts' (30/01/94), 'Home Thoughts' by Justine Picardie (16/1/94) and Yasmin Alibhai-Brown for 'Painful Guilt'; Crown copyright ('Poop the Scoop') is reproduced with the permission of the Controller of Her Majesty's Stationery Office; Harper Collins and Matt Groening for extracts from *Bart Simpson's Guide to Life*; Chronicle Books for extracts from *The Worst Case Scenario Survival Book* by Joshua Piven and David Bergenicht; *The Daily Mirror* and Jill Palmer for 'Why it's right to keep fighting for Jodie'; The Scott Polar Research Institute and UK/Bridgeman Art Library for 'Diary Entry for 9th January, 1902', 'Sledge hauling on the Great Ice Barrier, 1903' and 'Antarctic Sledging' all by Edward Adrian Wilson. Hodder and Stoughton Limited for extracts from *Misery* and *On Writing* by Stephen King; Fantagraphics Books and Joe Sacco for *Gorazde* (www.fantagraphics.com/preview/gorazde/gorazde.html); Giang Vo for 'Giang Vo's Story'.

Every effort has been made to trace and acknowledge copyright but if any accidental infringement has been made we would welcome information to redress the situation.

Contents

Introduction

Aims

The Non-Fiction Book is part of the new EMC KS3 Series for 11 – 14 year olds. Written to address the requirements of the National Curriculum and the *Framework for Teaching English, Years 7 – 9*, it is a pupil book which aims to provide stimulating, surprising and thought-provoking texts and activities on non-fiction. Activities are structured to fit approximately one hour lessons and each unit is designed to last between two and four weeks. The units aim to foreground the following elements of effective teaching:
- a fast pace and strong focus
- varied teaching styles and pupil groupings
- active approaches to texts
- shared reading and writing
- guided reading and writing.

Balancing range and progression

The book offers a choice of up to four units for each year. Taken as a whole, these texts and activities cover a wide range of non-fiction text types and teaching objectives, building progression into the skills of speaking, listening, reading and writing over a three year course. The order of the units in the pupil book reflect this sense of progression. Although units have been devised to address the different objectives of Years 7, 8 and 9, no mention is made of the Framework in the pupil book and units are not allocated to a particular year. This information is provided in the Teachers' notes on the CD Rom.

Teachers' notes

To support the teaching of these units, teachers' notes consist of:
- long, medium and short term plans for each unit, written to the Framework
- additional language notes
- pupil charts
- copies of some key texts, to allow for photocopying and annotation. These can also be made into OHTs for whole class work.

For maximum flexibility these notes are published on a CD ROM so that they can be printed off or amended as required. Updates in response to changes in national policy will be published on the English and Media Centre's free website (www.englishandmedia.co.uk).

Additional support for teaching terminology can be found on the 'Standards' pages of the DfEE website (www.standards.dfee.gov.uk/literacy/glossary).

4

Chocolate

In this unit you will learn:
- about the conventions of the main non-fiction text types
- about the text types used by different school subjects
- how to write your own non-fiction text.

Purpose – what does the text have to do?

The main non-fiction text types   Class work

Texts written for different purposes (for example to provide information or to argue a point of view) are written in different ways. Listed below are five of the main types of non-fiction text:
- information
- recount
- instruction
- persuasion
- argument (discursive writing).

■ Briefly share examples of each kind of text, from your own experience. For each different type, talk about the following:
- who might read it
- why
- to work well as a text, what should it be like?

The example below shows the sort of thing you might write.

Information text – a train timetable
People read train timetables to find out specific pieces of information so they can organise their journeys. It needs to be clear, simple, logical and quick to read.

■ From your discussion, sum up what you already know about the differences between information, recount, explanation, instruction, persuasion and argument (discursive writing).

The features of different text types

In the boxes on page 6 are some of the typical features of different types of non-fiction text.
■ Read through the list and talk about any of the typical features you are not clear about.

Information texts:
- – use the present tense
- – are written in the third person
- – make clear how information is organised and linked
- – include examples
- – make clarity a priority.

Recounts:
- – are written in the past tense
- – are written in the 1st or 3rd person
- – have a clear chronology (follow the sequence of time)
- – use connectives which help the reader grasp the order of past events (for example, then, later, when, after).

Explanation texts:
- – are written in the present tense
- – are usually written in an impersonal voice
- – try to make clear how things work.

Instruction texts:
- – use imperative verbs (commands such as 'Take' or 'Put')
- – are clear and concise
- – are carefully sequenced and signposted
- – use connectives which help the reader follow stages (for example first, next, now).

Persuasive texts:
- – use syntax (or the order of words in a sentence) to emphasise key points
- – are closely connected with argument and often use logic
- – build towards a conclusion
- – use language and rhetorical techniques to win over the reader (for example repetition, metaphors, similes, alliteration and so on).

Argument (or discursive writing):
- – weighs up contrasting points
- – signposts the different points of view in the argument by using phrases such as, on the one hand … on the other hand, however and nevertheless
- – uses the language and rhetorical techniques of persuasive writing
- – often uses a more reasonable tone than persuasive texts do
- – is more objective than a persuasive text
- – looks at the subject from more than one point of view
- – sums up or clarify what's been said at every stage
- – uses complex sentence grammar because it's dealing with difficult ideas and logical steps in thinking.

Main text types

Tasting different texts on chocolate   Pair and class work
Six short extracts from texts about chocolate are printed on pages 7 to 9.

■   Skim read the extracts and try to decide what type, or types, of non-fiction text each one is. Use the lists of features on page 6 to help you.

The extracts may have more than one purpose and use the features of more than one type of non-fiction text. Often when we write, we have several purposes at once. For instance, a children's fact book will almost certainly be trying to entertain and explain, as well as give information.

■   Take responsibility for looking more closely at one of the texts. Make notes to show what you notice about the way it is written. You should think about *some* of the ideas suggested here.

- What is it about? (the subject)
- What is it for? (the purpose or purposes)
- Who is meant to read it? (the audience)
- What does it look like on the page? (the layout and presentation)
- What do you notice about the length and type of sentences? (the sentence grammar)
- What do you notice about the word choices?
- How does it start and finish? How are the ideas linked together? (the structure of the whole text)

1. Chocolate – Health Help or Risk?

Chocolate has been said to cause acne and tooth decay, and has a reputation for being a fattening, nutritionless food. On the other hand, chocolate is also known for being everything from an anti-depressant to an aphrodisiac. While there's still much we don't know about chocolate, recent research is helping us better understand how chocolate consumption affects our health.

The good news is that most of the bad effects of eating chocolate are either overstated or entirely false. Eating chocolate neither causes nor aggravates acne. Two studies – one by the Pennsylvania School of Medicine and another by the U.S. Naval Academy – showed that eating chocolate (or not eating it) did not produce any significant changes in the acne conditions of the study's participants. These results are further backed by research which shows that acne is not primarily linked to diet.

Chocolate also has not been proven to cause cavities or tooth decay. In fact, there are indications that the cocoa butter in the chocolate coats the teeth and may help protect them by preventing plaque from forming. The sugar in chocolate does contribute to cavities, but no more than the sugar in any other food.

Obviously, eating too much of any food may cause health problems. The cocoa butter in chocolate does contain saturated fat, which can increase blood cholesterol levels, and high cholesterol can contribute to heart disease. However, recent research at the University of California has found that chocolate carries high levels of chemicals known as phenolics, some of which may help lower the risk of heart disease.

'Health help or risk?' by Jim Spandaccini (1998)
from *The Sweet Lure of Chocolate* from the Exploratorium website

2. White Chocolate Fondu Recipe

WHITE CHOCOLATE FONDUE

Makes 1½ cups
100 g packet white
   marshmallows
125 g white chocolate
½ cup sweetened
   condensed milk
⅓ cup sour cream
1 teaspoon imitation
   vanilla essence
fresh fruit, for dipping

1. Cut marshmallows into small pieces.

2. Chop chocolate coarsely.

3. Put condensed milk in a small pan. Heat gently for 5 minutes. LOW HEAT

4. Add marshmallows. Stir until almost smooth. LOW HEAT

5. Add chocolate. Take pan off heat.

6. Beat until chocolate melts and sauce is smooth.

7. Add cream and vanilla. Stir gently.

8. To serve, put the sauce in a bowl. Dip fruit in and eat.

82

White Chocolate Fondue from *Kids Cookbook 2*

Main text types

3. Giralamo Benzoni 1541

I was upwards of a year in that country without ever being induced to taste this beverage; and when I passed through a tribe, if an Indian wished occasionally to give me some, he was very much surprised to see me refuse it, and went away laughing. But subsequently, wine failing, and unwilling to drink nothing but water, I did as others did. The flavour is somewhat bitter, but it satisfies and refreshes the body without intoxicating; the Indians esteem it above everything, wherever they are accustomed to it.

4. The Chocolate Book

The cocoa tree is a tropical plant that flourishes only in a narrow band round the centre of the earth, not more than 20 degrees north or south of the equator. The Spanish established cocoa plantations throughout their Central and South American colonies, as well as in the Caribbean and the Philippines in the course of the 16th and 17th centuries. In the late 17th century, the Dutch took cocoa trees to Indonesia and Ceylon, and to the islands of Fernando Po and Sao Tome, off the coast of equatorial Africa. From here, cocoa was introduced to the Gold Coast in the late 1870s, and today Ghana and Nigeria are the world's leading cocoa growers, Brazil being the next largest producer.   From *The Chocolate Book* by Helge Rubinstein

5. 'I'm a chocoholic'

Well, we had to get round to the subject of chocolate eventually, didn't we? Chocolate is nice, there is no denying that. And there is no reason why you have to give up the taste of chocolate even while you are slimming.

   The reason I know this is that almost everybody eats chocolate yet very many of these people are not overweight. The way to tame your chocolate 'addiction', to make it something you can contain within a reasonable diet, is to look at the people who eat chocolate and aren't fat on it – and see what they are doing that you are not, and vice versa.   From *Slim for Life* by Judith Wills

6.

From a box of
Lir chocolates

Summing up the differences between texts

■   Take it in turns to feed back your ideas. Talk about what is similar and different about each text.

Writing about chocolate   Homework

■   Choose one of the non-fiction types listed on page 5. Write a paragraph about chocolate including some of the main features of the type of writing you have chosen. Use the ideas suggested here to get you started:
-    a recount of a disastrous attempt to make chocolate brownies
-    a Health Education Council information leaflet on chocolate and teeth
-    a series of instructions explaining how to eat a chocolate bar
-    a magazine advert for a completely new kind of chocolate bar.

Writing and reading at school

Which subject is it?   Class work

One of the biggest changes in moving from primary to secondary school is having the curriculum split into different subjects, each with its own kinds of writing. In Year 7, you have to get used to the way each subject uses writing. This involves getting to know:
-    the way texts are laid out and presented
-    the purposes of the writing (instruction, information and so on)
-    the specialist words used in the subject
-    the way the sentences are structured
-    the way the whole text is organised.

The extracts below are all taken from school text books.
- Read each extract and talk about which subject you think it is taken from. Which of the 5 aspects of texts listed on page 10 did you use to help you decide?

---

1.   Boats and balloons

A boat floats on water because of the upthrust.

If the boat weighs 10 00 newtons then the water must give an upthrust of 10 000 newtons.

A boat will float higher or lower depending on the *density* of the water.

Salty sea-water is more dense than fresh-water, so a boat floats higher in the salty sea than in a fresh-water lake.

A hydrogen balloon can float in air because the air gives it a small upthrust.

2.

In an indoor athletics stadium, four laps of the track are run in an 800 metre race. An athlete ran the first lap in 24.9 seconds, the first two laps in 51.4 seconds and the first three laps in 78.9 seconds. Her time for 800 metres was 1 minute 46.5 seconds.
a) What were her times for the second, third and fourth laps?
b) Which was her fastest lap?

---

3.   Transport links in a rural area

There are few roads and no railways between North and South Wales (map C). In most of the region the main routes are next to the coast. Inland routes have to follow the flatter land of river valleys. It is often hard to get from one river valley to the next because of the high land between them (photo F, page 83). The main transport link within Wales is the M4 motorway (diagram D). It was built to link the main towns, ports and industries of South Wales. At the same time it by-passed the centres of big cities. In North Wales the A55 is a major transport link.

---

4.   Slaves

The Romans took slavery for granted. For them a country without slaves was uncivilised.

From the third century BC, slaves flooded into Rome. Most were prisoners of war. Julius Caesar's conquest of Gaul alone brought in half a million slaves in five years. They were sold in the great slave markets in Rome and in other cities.

Some slaves worked and lived in rich people's houses. Others worked in mines or on large farming estates. But they all had one thing in common. They were the property of their master. They had no rights at all.

Were slaves treated badly? The evidence in sources 8-17 should help you answer this question.

Investigating subject text books Group work and class work

■ Share out the subject text books your teacher has provided, or use the text books that happen to be in your schoolbag.

■ Each group should take responsibility for looking at one subject. Choose a page showing the kind of writing you think is most typical of what you are asked to read and write in this subject. Use a chart like the one below to help you make detailed notes on the layout, organisation and style of the page.

Features	Comment	Example
Purposes		
Layout and presentation		
Specialist words used in the subject		
The structure of the sentences		
The organisation of the whole page		

■ Prepare a short report on what you have learned about the text to give to the rest of the class.

Reading and writing at school

■ Take it in turns to report back to the rest of the class. Together, sum up the similarities and differences in the sorts of writing and reading you are asked to do at school.

Making a poster Homework

■ Make a poster showing all you have learned about the different types of non-fiction text. You could add to this poster as you learn more about the non-fiction texts used in different subjects.

Webwriting

In this unit you will learn:
- about the layout, organisation and language of websites
- about what makes a successful web page
- how to write an evaluation of a web page
- how to plan, design and write a web page of your own
- how to use punctuation and layout to make your meaning clear to a reader.

The world wide web – what's it all about?

What do you know about websites?   Pair and class work

Some of you may be very familiar with the Internet, others may hardly have used it at all.

■   Share what you already know about the Internet. You could talk about:
- your own experiences of using the web
- the different types of website you've come across, and the purpose of each one (for example, to sell something, to provide information, to entertain you)
- the reasons why you chose to use the Internet in the first place, rather than a reference book or a video
- some sites which you find particularly interesting or fun, and the reasons why you enjoyed them
- the different reasons a company, an individual or a school might choose to have a website.

■   Look closely at the Home Pages on pages 14 and 15. Use them as examples to help you brainstorm your ideas about the questions below.

- What do you think the purpose of each website is?
- What do these particular websites have in common, and in what ways are they different?
- What do you think websites can do that other forms of written information can't do?
- How is reading a website different from reading a magazine or newspaper?

Browsing the internet   Homework
■   Spend some time browsing the Internet at home, in school or in your local library. Make a note of two or three websites which you think are interesting, well designed or easy to use. Choose the site you like most and print out its Home Page. Annotate the print out with your ideas about why you think it is successful.

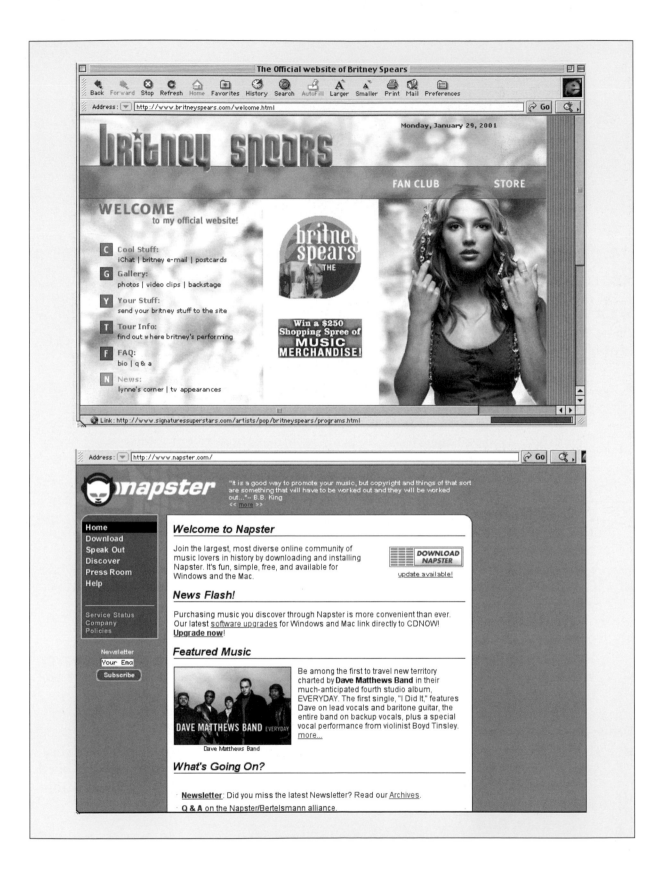

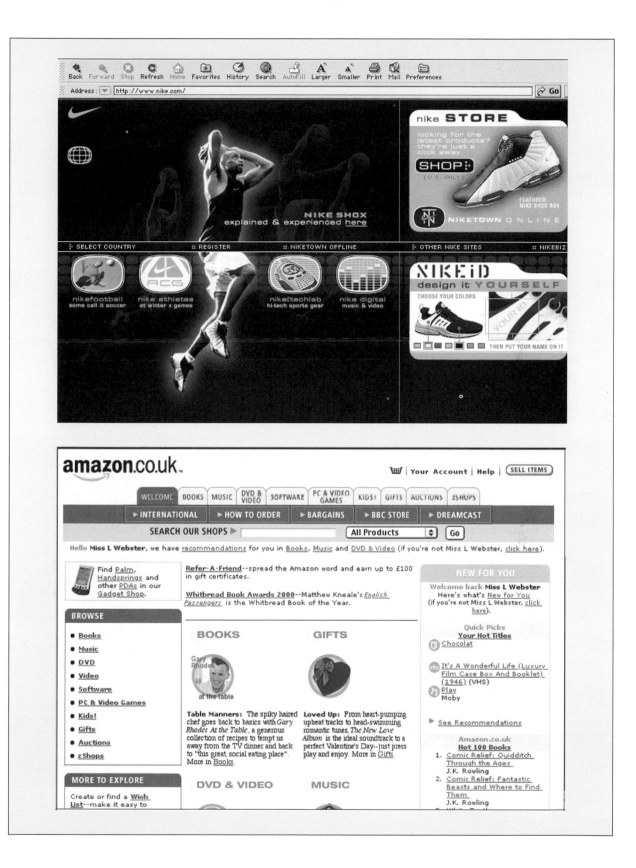

What makes a good Home Page?   Group and class work

■   In groups, take it in turns to introduce the Home Page you have each chosen. Agree three features you think make a successful Home Page.

■   Present your ideas about Home Pages to the rest of the class and draw together what you have learned so far.

Investigating a Home Page   Individual and pair work

For this activity, work either on the Home Page you introduced to the group or on one of those on pages 14 and 15.

Your web page will almost certainly contain a number of special Internet features.

■   Read the list below, and try to match each term with the correct definition.

■   Use the terms and the definitions to help you annotate the Home Page. In a different colour highlight or circle any other features you think are typical of a website and annotate them to show what they are for. (If you are using the examples on pages 14 and 15, you will need to write your notes on stickies.)

■   Compare what you have discovered with the person next to you.

A database of web pages which can be used to find particular information on the Internet.	an index
The clickable buttons or 'hot-spots' which connect different websites to each other.	a search engine
A space usually across the top of the screen reserved for advertising.	a logo
A graphic symbol, image or name associated with the website.	news items
The address of a website which tells you the name of the site, the sort of site it is, and (usually) its country of origin.	hyperlinks
A list of the topics and categories covered in the website.	a domain name
Small blocks of text summarising new information.	a banner

Analysing a Home Page – the look, design and layout Pair work

■ Talk about the overall 'look' of your page. Use the prompts suggested here to help you focus your analysis:
- the layout of the page (for example, how is the text broken up?)
- the use of colour or tone
- the use of illustration, images and other design features (for example, sound and animation)
- the type of font used
- the icons (for example, are they designed to help you to navigate the site and find the page or the information you really want?).

■ Draw a thumbnail sketch to show how the blocks of print and images fit together. The sketch included here shows you the sort of thing you might do.

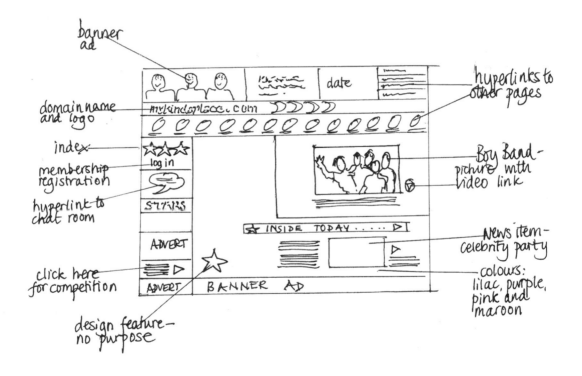

■ Annotate your sketch with your ideas about the way design features, colour, fonts and so on have been used and why. For example, fonts can be used to attract attention, communicate information clearly and give a site a particular image.

Evaluating a good Home Page   Class work
■   Compare your ideas with the rest of the class. Can you agree on any typical features or designs which make a good Home Page?

■   Use the phrases below to agree the features which make a good Home Page.

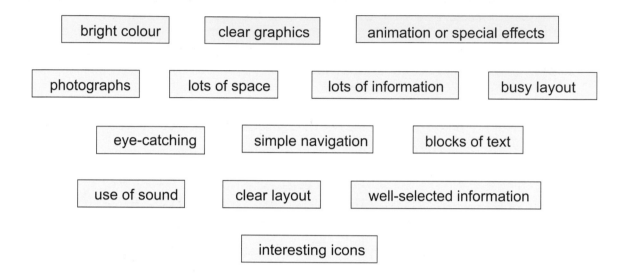

bright colour   clear graphics   animation or special effects

photographs   lots of space   lots of information   busy layout

eye-catching   simple navigation   blocks of text

use of sound   clear layout   well-selected information

interesting icons

Writing an evaluation   Homework
■   Write a short evaluation of a Home Page you particularly like. Look back at the list of prompts on page 17 to help you.

Designing your own website

A Year Seven Survival Guide   Class work
You have been asked by your school to design a 'Year 7 Survival Guide' to go on the school website.

■   Brainstorm your ideas about the possible contents of the 'Year 7 Survival Guide'. Think about the sort of things you would have liked to know before you started at the school. For example, what do I need to bring with me?

■   Use your class brainstorm to decide on four or five key topics which you think you should include in your web guide.

Planning your Home Page Individual and pair work

■   Use what you have learned so far to plan and sketch an attractive, reader-friendly Home Page for your 'Year Seven Survival Guide'. Your Home Page should let the 'reader' know what else can be found on the other pages of the site.

■   Annotate the sketch with your ideas about images, colour, fonts and other design features you could use. Very briefly indicate the reasons for your choices.

■   Work together to check your Home Page against the class criteria. Make any alterations which you think are needed.

Linking the Home Page

■   Show how the Home Page will link to other pages in your web guide by annotating your diagram in the way shown here.

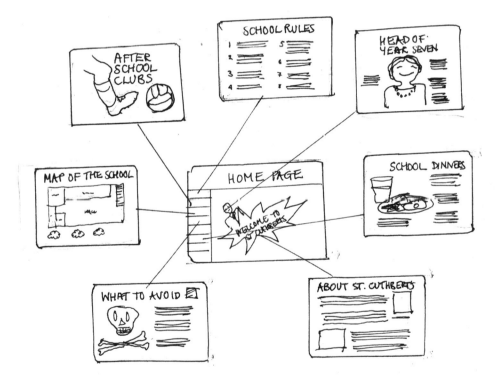

Whole class feedback

■   Take it in turns to feed back what you have learned about the organisation and layout of a Home Page.

Writing on the web Homework

■   Make a note of three things you have noticed about the style of writing and language used on a website. In what ways is the style of writing similar to, or different from a book or magazine?

Writing for the web

Advice from the experts Class work

■ Share your ideas about the style of writing you think is most suitable for the Internet.

The three extracts below and on the next page are taken from websites giving advice to people who write for the web.

■ Listen to the advice being read out loud and jot down any points you think are particularly helpful or important.

■ Use the advice to work out a set of guidelines for writing for the web. Write down your guidelines under the headings suggested here.

– When writing for the web, you should:
– When writing for the web, you should avoid:

1. People on the web have short attention spans.

- Keep words, sentences and paragraphs short.
- Use sub-headings to break up and summarise text.
- Use lists wherever possible.
- Only include information which is really necessary.
- When appropriate, use drawings, photographs, animation and so on.

www.phillynews.com/inquirer.htm

2. Organise the information

- Sort information into clearly labelled groups. Divide each group into sub-groups.
- Layout similar information in the same way.
- Writing is 'chunked' into bite size pieces. Headings, sub-headings and sub-sub-headings work as clear labels for each chunk. Items in lists are bulleted or numbered (easier to scan).
- When moving a printed text to a website, reduce the number of words by 50%.
- Use few words and short sentences.
- Don't write like you talk.

www.ronscheer.com

Presentation and structure

3. Visitors don't read your page, they browse it.

A well written web page should read more like a brochure or a briefing than a formal report.
- Reduce your word count. Terse pages are easier to read than long pages.
- Use one idea per paragraph. Ideas buried inside a paragraph are often missed.
- Use bullet lists, bold text and sub-headings to highlight key points.
- Write using an 'inverted pyramid' style, placing the most important ideas at the top of your page.
- Avoid clutter.

www.netmechanic.com

A school brochure
The extract below is from a school brochure for Year 7 pupils.
- ■   Listen to the extract being read out loud and talk about your first responses to it.

Congratulations - you're preparing for the daunting prospect of starting your new secondary school at last! You're probably full of anticipation, but many students will also be experiencing feelings of terror - especially if they are the eldest and have no older siblings to teach them the ropes. From circumnavigating the maze-like and crowded building - a nightmare if you missed the guided tour - to deciding whether to choose packed lunch or school dinners (chips, chips and more chips!), you will be faced with a bewildering array of choices, decisions, and new situations.

So how do you start getting to know your way around? What are your options if you can't find the right classroom? What if you misplace your timetable or don't understand the homework? We know that all new pupils share these sorts of worries; this booklet aims to put your mind at rest and show you how to survive, make the most of and even enjoy the exciting new experience that is your secondary school. Welcome!

Your first port of call in the school is your tutor room, which is the place where you register every morning. You will be in one of 8 tutor groups which are supervised by your Head of Year, who is responsible for all the students in your year. However, your Form Tutor is the member of staff who will be responsible for your welfare right the way through the school from Year 7 to Year 11, both in terms of your school work and your social life. Your tutor is also the person to whom you should go with any problems, no matter how trifling they may seem. Your tutor's main job is to get to know you very well. You will meet each other twice daily to check on routine matters such as attendance. Your form teacher will also teach the Personal, Social and Health Education Programme (PSHE) which aims to make you a happy, secure and confident member of the school community who respects and cares for others.

Practise 'webwriting' – editing an article   Pair and class work

- Your job is to develop your webwriting skills by editing the article for a web page. The web page should:
- be informative
- include the main points of the article
- be easy to read and understand
- include no more than four hyperlinks to other pages or sections
- use only two images.

- Spend a couple of minutes scanning the text. Talk about what makes it unsuitable for a website. Choose two things which you think would be a particular problem if this article was put on a website as it is. Look back at your class guidelines on writing for the web and think about how you could overcome these problems.

- Collect together all the different ways in which this text is not suitable for the web.

- A few of the criticisms you may have mentioned, and some of the ways the text could be changed, are suggested here. How could you overcome some of the other problems you noticed?

Problem	Solution
Long boring sentences	Put key point in a heading List additional information as bullet points
Difficult to scan	Break the text into smaller chunks Use sub-headings
Boring to look at	Add some images and some different fonts and colours Use cartoons or photographs to give some of the information

Presentation and structure

Editing the article   Individual and class work

■ Have a go at editing the extract for a school website. Your teacher will give you a photocopy for you to mark up in the following way:
- underline the points which would make good headings for chunks of text
- in another colour, underline where you could use a hyperlink
- put an arrow by any section which you think could be replaced by an illustration or cartoon
- draw a line through anything you think could be cut
- put asterisks or stars beside points which could be listed as bullet points.

■ Experiment with re-drafting a paragraph or two. Here is the way one pupil analysed and re-drafted the first paragraph.

Too long - Needs a snappier intro

Too long winded and scary

Congratulations - you're preparing for the daunting prospect of starting your new secondary school at last! You're probably full of anticipation, but many students will also be experiencing feelings of terror - especially if they are the eldest and have no older siblings to act as role models and teach them the ropes. From circumnavigating the maze-like and crowded building - a nightmare if you missed the guided tour - to deciding whether to choose packed lunch or school dinners (chips, chips and more chips!), you will be faced with a bewildering array of choices, decisions, and new situations.

Why so complicated?

Give it a bold title - a question to grab the readers attention

Starting Year Seven?

Exciting, isn't it – but don't worry if you're a bit scared too! There's a lot to learn – what you need, how to get around the building, the rules, whether to have sandwiches or school grub, and loads more.

No need to give as many details - could include a link to another page

Re-written versions
■ Listen to a few of the re-written versions and talk about what makes them more successful than the original.

Writing your own web pages

You have already sketched out your Home Page with its links to the rest of your web guide. Your task now is to write the 'inside' pages of your guide.

- Recap what you have learned about the following features of a website:
  - organisation
  - styles of writing
  - layout and design.

Planning and writing the web guide   Group and individual work

- Use your Home Pages to help you decide on the content (for example, the introduction, first day, lessons, after school clubs and so on) and the overall structure of the web guide. You could collect together your ideas in the form of a spider diagram.

- Talk together about the style and layout of your website. You will need to agree on:
  - colour
  - style of fonts
  - design of icons and buttons
  - use of sub-headings
  - use of graphics
  - amount of information to be included on each page.
  - ways to make the page easy to scan.

Drafting a web page

- Each person should take responsibility for working on one of the pages.

- Draft a rough plan of your web page. Experiment with different ways of organising the main blocks of information. Sketch in the main sections, with headings and sub-headings. Think about how you are going to link the blocks of information and guide the reader through the different sections.

- Write a first draft of the text of your web page.

Discussing the drafts

- Take it in turns to present your draft web page to the group.

- Use the class guidelines to help you evaluate each web page and to suggest ways in which it could be altered. Is it suitable for the purpose and audience? You should think about the content, the layout and the style of writing.

Group reports
■   Take it in turns to give a very brief report on the progress of each group's web guide.

A final draft   Homework
■   Taking into account the comments of the group, do a final draft of your web page.

Group presentations of your work

Presenting your work   Class and group work
■   Draw up a list of what you should include in your presentation of the web guides (for example, your aims, the content, the reasons for your decisions, whether or not it is a successful example of writing for the Internet).

■   Talk about what makes a successful presentation.

■   Prepare a two minute presentation of your web guide.

■   Take it in turns to give your group presentations of your web guides.

Writing a commentary   Homework
■   Write a short commentary on your group web guide. You should think about:
-     what you were trying to do
-     how you tried to do this
-     how successful you think you have been
-     what you have learned in this unit.

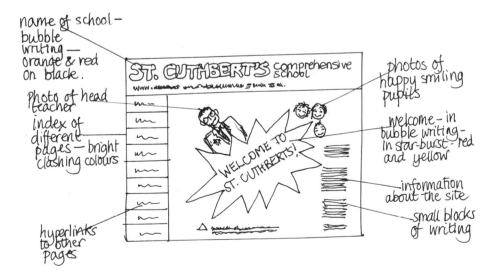

Do not...

In this unit you will:
- learn about how instruction texts are structured and the language they use
- read and analyse texts which use the conventions of instruction texts
- write your own instruction text which is easy to follow and clearly sequenced
- use detail, examples and diagrams to illustrate your meaning
- read and analyse a text which offers advice
- read a send-up of an advice leaflet and write your own.

Getting the message across

Comparing texts   Class work

The writers of the texts on page 27 all use language and layout (for example, spacing, different letters, numbering) to help them get their message across to their audience.

■   Talk about any similarities and differences you notice between the texts. You could think about:
-   length
-   how formal or informal the text is
-   the 'tone' of the message
-   the order of the different pieces of information in the message
-   the way the different pieces of information are joined together
-   what's interesting about the use of verbs.

■   How does the subject matter, audience and purpose of each text affect the way it has been written?

Writing to instruct and advise

Dear Chloe,
Don't, don't, don't send that letter! It's not the end of the world and the sooner
you realise that the better. Go out, have fun, GET A LIFE — he may begin to see
that you're worth a lot more than he realises. Good luck!
Auntie Amy

Go directly to jail.
Do not pass Go.
Do not collect £200.

FIRE SAFETY NOTICE

Familiarise yourself with the layout of the emergency exits
and safety equipment.

In case of fire:
- Do not panic.
- Close all doors.
- Raise the alarm. Alarms are situated in three places on
  each floor, directly opposite the lift and at either end of
  the corridor.
- Find the nearest emergency exit.
- Do not use the lift.

How to help us provide an efficient service for you

Do ring if you can't keep your appointment.

Do wait patiently if the surgery is busy.

Do make a list of everything you want to ask the doctor.

Do ask to see the nurse for routine matters, such as vaccinations, changes of dressing and so on.

Don't ask for a home call, unless you really are too sick to attend surgery.

Don't leave the surgery while you're waiting to see a doctor, without letting the receptionist know.

Don't ring on Thursday afternoons unless it is an emergency.

The surgery is closed between 1 p.m. and 6.00 p.m.

Thank you.

Dr. Williams, Dr. Ahmed, Dr. Scott

Writing to instruct and advise   Pair and class work

Instruction and advice texts often use the following:

- the present tense
- imperative verbs (These are verbs which give orders, for example 'Take', 'Start' and so on.)
- clear and concise guidance (no unnecessary padding)
- details, examples, diagrams or illustrations
- appealing and accessible presentation
- clearly sequenced lists
- signposts to the reader, such as bold sub-heads, bullet points and numbered points.

■   Take responsibility for looking closely at one text and look for examples of these features.

What did you notice?

■   Take it in turns to report back at least three features that you found.

How to ... escape from quicksand

The Worst Case Scenario Survival Handbook gives advice on how to survive the most extreme situations, for example how to escape from a crocodile, deliver a baby in a car and survive a shipwreck. These texts demonstrate the typical features of instruction texts in humorous ways.

■   Read the instructions on 'How to ... escape from quicksand' below, then talk about which features of instruction texts it demonstrates. Look at the original illustrations on the next page.

How to Escape from Quicksand

1. When walking in quicksand country, carry a stout pole - it will help you get out should you need to.
2. As soon as you start to sink, lay the pole on the surface of the quicksand.
3. Flop onto your back on top of the pole.
   After a minute or two, equilibrium in the quicksand will be achieved, and you will no longer sink.
4. Work the pole to a new position under your hips, and at right angles to your spine.
   The pole will keep your hips from sinking, as you (slowly) pull out first one leg, and then the other.
5. Take the shortest route to firmer ground, moving slowly.

How to Avoid Sinking

Quicksand is just ordinary sand mixed with upwelling water, which makes it behave like a liquid. However, quicksand - unlike water - does not easily let go. If you try to pull a limb out of quicksand, you have to work against the vacuum left behind. Here are a few tips:

♦   The viscosity of quicksand increases with shearing - move slowly so the viscosity is as low as possible.
♦   Floating on quicksand is relatively easy and is the best way to avoid its clutches. You are more buoyant in quicksand than you are in water. Humans have a specific gravity just under 1.00, while fresh water has a specific gravity of 1.00. Saltwater is slightly more dense at 1.02, and floating is significantly easier in saltwater than in freshwater. Spread your arms and legs far apart and try to float on your back.

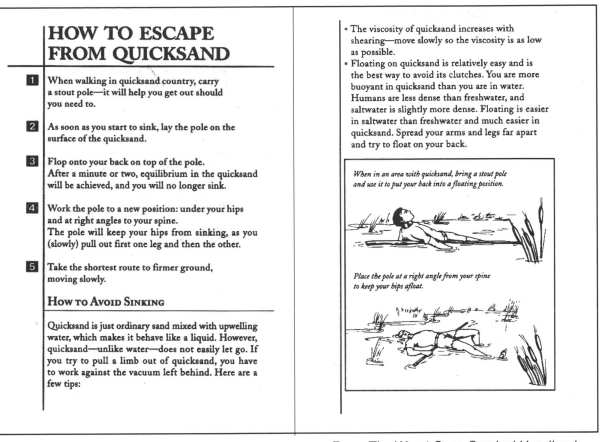

HOW TO ESCAPE FROM QUICKSAND

1 When walking in quicksand country, carry a stout pole—it will help you get out should you need to.

2 As soon as you start to sink, lay the pole on the surface of the quicksand.

3 Flop onto your back on top of the pole. After a minute or two, equilibrium in the quicksand will be achieved, and you will no longer sink.

4 Work the pole to a new position: under your hips and at right angles to your spine. The pole will keep your hips from sinking, as you (slowly) pull out first one leg and then the other.

5 Take the shortest route to firmer ground, moving slowly.

How to Avoid Sinking

Quicksand is just ordinary sand mixed with upwelling water, which makes it behave like a liquid. However, quicksand—unlike water—does not easily let go. If you try to pull a limb out of quicksand, you have to work against the vacuum left behind. Here are a few tips:

- The viscosity of quicksand increases with shearing—move slowly so the viscosity is as low as possible.
- Floating on quicksand is relatively easy and is the best way to avoid its clutches. You are more buoyant in quicksand than you are in water. Humans are less dense than freshwater, and saltwater is slightly more dense. Floating is easier in saltwater than freshwater and much easier in quicksand. Spread your arms and legs far apart and try to float on your back.

When in an area with quicksand, bring a stout pole and use it to put your back into a floating position.

Place the pole at a right angle from your spine to keep your hips afloat.

From *The Worst Case Survival Handbook*

What have you learned?

■ Feed back your observations on the 'How to' text and sum up what you have learned about writing to instruct.

A survival guide   Homework

■ Now try writing your own short 'How to...' text including as many of the features from the list on page 28 as you can. Choose one of the following tasks.

- Choose one of the topics from the Contents Page of *The Worst Case Scenario Survival Handbook* on page 30.
- Make up a topic of your own, for instance, 'How to get out of household chores'.
- Write the instructions to go with the images on page 30 showing how to 'Cut and Paste' on a computer. You must explain every single action in language which is simple and clear enough for someone who has no knowledge of computers to understand.

Worst-Case Scenario Survival Handbook – Table of contents

How to Survive a Poisonous Snake Attack

How to Survive Adrift at Sea

How to Escape a from a Bear

How to Survive When Lost in the Desert

How to Wrestle Free from an Alligator

How to Survive an Avalanche

How to Deal with a Charging Bull

How to Survive When Lost in the Mountains

How to Win a Sword Fight

How to Make Fire Without Matches

How to Survive an Earthquake

How to Avoid Being Stuck by Lightning

How to 'Cut and paste'.

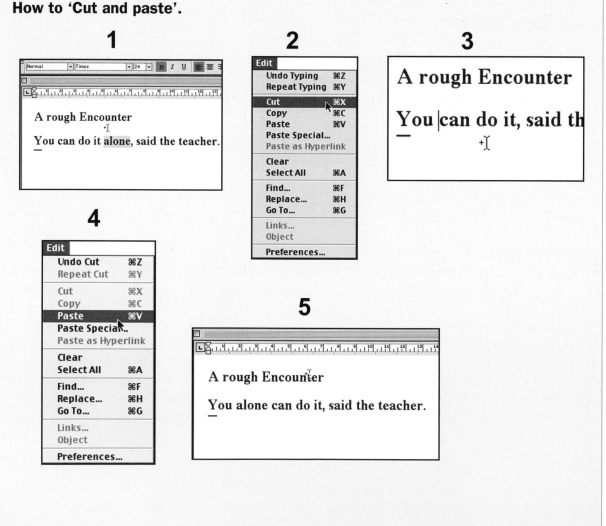

Giving advice – side effects

A patient information leaflet   Pair and class work

Triludan used to be available over the counter in chemists but after some serious side effects were reported, it became available only through prescription. It has now been withdrawn completely!

Reading the advice leaflet

■   Take it in turns to read aloud the Triludan Patient Information Leaflet below and on the next page. How easy or difficult do you find it to read and understand? Can you sum up the purpose of this text in just one sentence?

■   Look back at the list of features used in texts which instruct and advise (page 28). Make notes showing which of these features the Triludan Patient Information Leaflet uses.

Talking about 'Triludan'

.
■   Compare your notes and talk about what you notice that's unusual or interesting about this leaflet, as an example of an instruction or advice text. For instance, you could think about why it is so long. Why isn't it as concise as you might expect an instruction text to be?

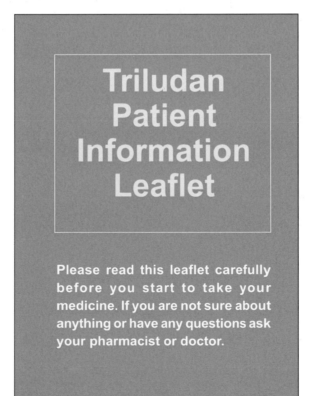

Triludan
Patient
Information
Leaflet

Please read this leaflet carefully before you start to take your medicine. If you are not sure about anything or have any questions ask your pharmacist or doctor.

Triludan is an antihistamine. Antihistamines relieve the symptoms such as sneezing, watery eyes, blocked or runny nose, that occur with hayfever (seasonal allergic rhinitis) and a similar condition called perennial rhinitis that continues throughout the year.

They also relieve the redness, swelling and itching of some allergic skin complaints including nettlerash and reactions to insect bites and stings. In some circumstances it is very important not to take Triludan and these are listed below. If you ignore these instructions, this medicine could affect your heart rhythm.

DO NOT take Triludan if you are taking:
- azole antifungals (medicines for fungus infections), for example, ketoconazole and itraconazole
- macrolide antibiotics, for example erythromycin

These will have been prescribed by a doctor and sometimes are known by other names.

Also DO NOT take Triludan if you
- know that you have a liver problem
- have an abnormal heart tracing (ECG)
- have abnormal blood electrolyte levels (sodium, potassium, magnesium)

You should avoid drinking grapefruit juice before or after taking Triludan.

Tests show that Triludan does not cause drowsiness so that you can usually drive while you are on treatment with Triludan. However there may be rare exceptions so make sure that you are not affected in this way before driving or carrying out tasks requiring concentration.

Take your tablets with water. You may take them with or without food. Triludan should not be taken with grapefruit juice.

Adults and children over 12 years:
Hayfever, allergic rhinitis: One tablet once daily or half a tablet twice daily. Increase to two tablets once daily or one tablet twice daily if required.
Allergic skin conditions:
One tablet twice daily. Alternatively, two tablets may be taken once daily.

Children:
Hayfever, allergic rhinitis, allergic skin conditions:
6 to 12 years:
Half a tablet twice daily.
Do not take more than the maximum dose recommended above.
If you accidentally take too many tablets, ask your doctor for advice at once or go to the nearest hospital casualty department.
If you miss a tablet do not take extra to make up, but continue with the next dose as usual.
If the tablets do not work DO NOT take extra tablets: tell your doctor or pharmacist.
Most people have no side effects with Triludan but as with all medicines it may not suit everyone. There may occasionally be problems although these are rare.
 If you get any of the following stop taking the tablets and tell your pharmacist or doctor straight away:-
- Fits, fainting and/or palpitations [pounding heart]
- Unexpected swelling, particularly around the face and throat

- Tight chest or wheezing
Other possible side effects are:
- Stomach pain and upset
- Headache or dizziness
- Disturbed sleep/nightmares
- Hair loss
- Rash/sunlight sensitivity/itchiness
- Depression or confusion
- Liver problems/jaundice (yellowing of the skin and the whites of the eyes)
- Menstrual problems
- Aches and pains/pins & needles
- Sweating/trembling
- Sight disturbance
- Bruising
- Tiredness (fatigue)
- Breast discomfort (milk production)
- Increased urinary frequency (you may pass water more often)
- Heart beat irregularities

If you notice anything else unusual or have any unexpected effects, tell your pharmacist or doctor.

Reading 'Side Effects' by Steve Martin

The comedian Steve Martin has written a send-up of patient information leaflets like the Triludan example.

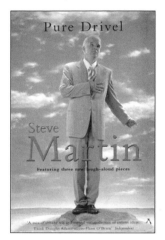

Steve Martin is an American comedian who has appeared in many films such as *Roxanne, Airplane, Father of the Bride and The Jerk*. 'Side Effects' is published in a collection of his writing called *Pure Drivel* which *The Mirror* describes as 'off-the-wall, sharp … He drops bizarre words, confetti-like, all over the place.'

What makes it funny? Class and pair work

■ Listen to 'Side Effects' being read aloud and share your first thoughts about what makes it funny.

Side Effects

Dosage: Take two tablets every six hours for joint pain.

Side effects: This drug may cause joint pain, nausea, headache, or shortness of breath. You may also experience muscle aches, rapid heartbeat, or ringing in the ears. If you feel faint, call your doctor. Do not consume alcohol while taking this pill; likewise, avoid red meat, shellfish, and vegetables. Okay foods: flounder. Under no circumstances eat yak … Projectile vomiting is common in 30 percent of users - sorry: 50 percent. If you undergo disorienting nausea accompanied by migraine with audible raspy breathing, double the dosage. Leg cramps are to be expected; up to one knee-buckler per day is allowable. Bowel movements may become frequent, in fact every ten minutes. If bowel movements become greater than twelve per hour, consult your doctor, or in fact any doctor, or anyone who will speak to you. You may find yourself becoming lost or vague; this would be a good time to write a screenplay. Do not pilot a plane, unless you are in the 10 percent of users who experience 'spontaneous test pilot knowledge.' If your hair begins to smell like burning tyres, move away from any buildings or populated areas and apply tincture of iodine to the head until you no longer hear what could be considered to be a 'countdown'. May cause stigmata in Mexicans. Do not sit on pointy conical objects. If a fungus starts to grow between your eyebrows, call the *Guinness Book of Records*. Do not operate heavy machinery, especially if you feel qualified for a desk job; that's good advice anytime … It is advisable to have a friend handcuff you to a large kitchen appliance, ESPECIALLY ONE THAT WILL NOT FIT THROUGH THE DOORWAY TO WHERE THE PILLS ARE.

Looking more closely at 'Side effects' Pair and class work

■ Pick out one or two short quotations which you find particularly amusing and, in your own words, explain what makes them funny. Share your quotations with the person next to you.

■ Use a chart like the one below to help you see which features of patient information leaflets Steve Martin uses.

■ How does he make fun of these features at the same time as using them?

Features of the Triludan leaflet	Example from 'Side Effects'
Present tense	
Imperative verbs (giving orders)	
Details, examples, diagrams or illustrations	
Clearly sequenced lists	
Signposts to the reader	
Emphasises the advice	

Write your own send-up Homework

■ Write your own send-up to show what you have learned about the typical features of texts which aim to instruct and advise. Local libraries are a good place to look for leaflets like this. To make it funny you need to stay close to the way this type of text is typically written.

■ Annotate your work to show which features of an instruction/advice text you are making fun of and how.

Captain Scott

In this unit you will:
- look closely at a famous literary non-fiction text
- learn about how the purpose, audience and form of this text affected the way it was written
- use this text as the basis of an information text book.

What sort of writing is this?

Exploring fragments of text   Class and pair work

■   Your teacher will read four fragments of text to you. As you listen, jot down your first response to each one. For example, you might have some ideas about the type of writing it is, who might have written it and why.

■   Read the fragments and make very brief notes about each one. Some of the things you could think about as you read are suggested here:
-   the sort of writing it is
-   why it was written (the purpose)
-   who it was written for (the audience)
-   the way it is written (for example, in a formal or chatty style; in notes or full sentences)
-   your personal opinion of it.

■   Take it in turns to share your ideas with the rest of the class.

1.   The sun with blurred image peeping shyly through the wreathing drift giving pale shadowless light. The eternal silence of the great white desert. Cloudy columns of snow drift advancing from the south, pale yellow wraiths, heralding the coming storm, blotting out one by one the sharp-cut lines of the land …

2.   Friday, 16 March or Saturday, 17
Lost track of dates, but think the last correct

3.   I take this opportunity of saying that we have stuck to our sick companions to the last … We knew that poor Oates was walking to his death, but though we tried to dissuade him, we knew it was the act of a brave man and an English gentleman.

> **4.** Blizzard bad as ever – Wilson and Bowers unable to start – tomorrow last chance – no fuel and only one or two of food left – must be near the end.

All four fragments are taken from the diary of Captain Scott. This diary was written during his expedition to the South Pole in 1912. Although Scott and his team reached the Pole on 18th January 1912, they died at the end of March, on their way back to the base camp. The diary was discovered with the frozen bodies of the men nine months later, in November 1912.

Diary entry for 9th January 1902

Reading the diary   Class and individual work

■   Read the fragments for a second time. Does the information about where they are taken from change the way you respond to them? If so, in what ways?

■   Listen to the whole extract being read out loud.

Literary non-fiction

The Diary of Captain Scott

Impressions

The seductive folds of the sleeping-bag.

The hiss of the primus and the fragrant steam of the cooker issuing from the tent ventilator.

The small green tent and the great white road.

The whine of a dog and the neigh of our steeds.

The driving cloud of powdered snow.

The crunch of footsteps which break the surface crust.

The wind-blown furrows.

The blue arch beneath the smoky cloud.

The crisp ring of the ponies' hoofs and the swish of the following sledge.

The droning conversation of the march as driver encourages or chides his horse.

The patter of dog pads.

The gentle flutter of our canvas shelter.

Its deep booming sound under the full force of blizzard.

The drift snow like finest flour penetrating every hole and corner – flickering up beneath one's head covering, pricking sharply as a sand blast.

The sun with blurred image peeping shyly through the wreathing drift giving pale shadowless light. The eternal silence of the great white desert. Cloudy columns of snow drift advancing from the south,pale yellow wraiths, heralding the coming storm, blotting out one by one the sharp-cut lines of the land …

Friday, 16 March or Saturday, 17. Lost track of dates, but think the last correct. Tragedy all along the line. At lunch, the day before yesterday, poor Titus Oates said he couldn't go on; he proposed we should leave him in his sleeping-bag. That we could not do, and induced him to come on, on the afternoon march. In spite of its awful nature for him he struggled on and we made a few miles. At night he was worse and we knew the end had come.

Should this be found I want these facts recorded. Oates's last thoughts were of his Mother, but immediately before he took pride in thinking that his regiment would be pleased with the bold way in which he met his death. We can testify to his bravery. He has borne intense suffering for weeks without complaint, and to the very last was able and willing to discuss outside subjects. He did not - would not -give up hope to the very end. He was a brave soul. This was the end. He slept through the night before last, hoping not to wake; but he woke in the morning – yesterday. It was blowing a blizzard. He said, 'I am just going outside and may be some time' and we have not seen him since.

I take this opportunity of saying that we have stuck to our sick companions to the last. In the case of Edgar Evans, when absolutely out of food and he lay insensible, the safety of the remainder seemed to demand his abandonment, but Providence mercifully removed him at this critical moment. He died a natural death, and we did not leave him till two hours after his death. We knew that poor Oates was walking to his death, but though we tried to dissuade him, we knew it was the act of a brave man and an English gentleman. We all hope to meet the end with a similar spirit, and assuredly the end is not far.

I can only write at lunch and then only occasionally. The cold is intense, -40° at midday. My companions are unendingly cheerful, but we are all on the verge of serious frostbites, and though we talk constantly of fetching through I don't think any one of us feels it in his heart.

We are cold on the march now, and at all times except meals. Yesterday we had to lay up for a blizzard and today we move dreadfully slowly. We are at No. 14 pony camp, only two pony marches on from One Ton Depot. We leave here our theodolite, a camera and Oates's sleeping-bags.

Diaries etc., and geological specimens carried at Wilson's special request, will be found with us on our sledge.

Sunday, 18 March
Today, lunch, we are 21 miles from the depot. Ill fortune presses, but better may come. We have had more wind and drift from ahead yesterday; had to stop marching; wind N.W., force 4, temp. -35°. No human being could face it, and we are worn out *nearly*.
My right foot has gone, nearly all the toes - two days ago I was proud possessor of best feet. These are the steps of my downfall. Like an ass I mixed a small spoonful of curry powder with my melted pemmican – it gave me violent indigestion. I lay awake and in pain all night; woke and felt done on the march; foot went and didn't know it. A very small measure of neglect and have a foot which is not pleasant to contemplate. Bowers takes first place in condition, but there is not much to choose after all. The others are still confident of getting through – or pretend to be – I don't know! We have the last *half* fill of oil in our primus and a very small quantity of spirit – this alone between us and thirst. The wind is fair for the moment, and this is perhaps a fact to help. The mileage would have seemed ridiculously small on our outward journey.

Monday, 19 March
Lunch. We camped with difficulty last night and were dreadfully cold till after our supper of cold pemmican and biscuit and a half pannikin of cocoa cooked over the spirit. Then, contrary to expectation, we got warm and all slept well. Today we started in the usual dragging manner. Sledge dreadfully heavy. We are 15 miles from the depot and ought to get there in three days. What progress! We have two days' food but barely a day's fuel. All our feet are getting bad – Wilson's best, my right foot worse, left all right. There is no chance to nurse one's feet till we can get hot food into us. Amputation is the least I can hope for now, but will the trouble spread? That is the serious question. The weather doesn't give us a chance – the wind from N. to N.W. and -40° today.

Wednesday, 21 March
Got within 11 miles of depot Monday night; had to lay up all yesterday in severe blizzard. Today forlorn hope, Wilson and Bowers going to depot for fuel.

Thursday 22nd and 23 March
Blizzard as bad as ever - Wilson and Bowes unable to start - tomorrow last chance. No fuel and only one or two of food left – must be near the end. Have decided it shall be natural – we shall march for the depot with or without our effects and die in our tracks.

Thursday, 29 March
Since the 21st we have had a continuous gale from W.S.W and S.W. We had fuel to make two cups of tea apiece and bare food for two days on the 20th. Every day we have been ready to start for our depot *11 miles away,* but outside the door of the tent it remains a whirling drift. I do not think we can hope for better things now. We shall stick it out to the end, but we are getting weaker, of-course, and the end cannot be far.
  It seems a pity but I do not think I can write more.
R. Scott
For God's sake look after our people.

■   Talk about anything which strikes you as important or interesting on this first full reading. You could use the questions suggested here to focus your thinking.

–   Why do you think Scott wrote this diary?
–   Who do you think he wrote it for?
–   What is it about the content or style of the diary which suggests this to you?

■   Share your thoughts with the rest of the class.

What was Captain Scott like?   Homework
■   Read the full extract from the diary again, and write down three things you discover about the character of Captain Scott.

Creating character

What sort of man was Captain Scott?   Pair and class work
■   Tell each other what you have discovered about Captain Scott. Pick out the sections of the diary which gave you these impressions of Scott.

Sledge hauling in the Great Ice Barrier 1903

- Feed back the main points of your discussion on Captain Scott. What sort of person was he? What was important to him?

- Take it in turns to suggest adjectives which you think describe his character.

- Choose a short quotation to illustrate each word. You could set out your work in the way shown here.

Captain Scott

Brave ('Amputation is the least I can hope for now')

Concerned ('At lunch, the day before yesterday, poor Titus Oates said he couldn't go on')

Writing about Captain Scott   Individual and class work

- Write two or three sentences about Captain Scott.

- Experiment with different ways of joining together the individual descriptions. Some connectives for you to try out are suggested here.

| However | And | In addition | Also |
| On the other hand | | Moreover | |

A class character sketch

- Use your individual descriptions to write a class character sketch of Captain Scott. Begin by collecting together five or six different sentences. Your teacher will write these for you on the board or OHT.

- Take it in turns to suggest different ways these sentences could be joined together. Talk about the ways which seem to you to be most appropriate or most effective.

A description of Captain Scott   Individual and class work

- Write a short description of Captain Scott. Use your own draft sentences and the class model to help you.

Literary non-fiction

Purpose and audience

Why write a diary?   Class and Individual work
- Make a list of all the different reasons someone might write a diary.

Many diaries are entirely private and remain so. The diaries of some people are published after they are dead. Other people write diaries with the intention of publishing them. Captain Scott's Diary is both a personal and public account. Scott knew that this would be an important part of history. He wanted the diary to record his experiences for future readers.

A personal and public diary
- Find one section which you think was written with a future reader in mind. Now find a section which seems to you to be more personal.

- Take it in turns to feed back the personal and public sections you identified.

- Talk about the similarities and differences between the two sections you identified. You should think about both the subject matter and the style of the writing.

Talking about purpose and audience
- How does purpose and audience of a piece of writing influence the content and the style of the writing? Talk about what you have noticed.

What was important to Scott?   Homework
- What ideas do you get about the society Scott belonged to? For instance, can you tell anything about the values or beliefs of both Scott and the people he was writing for?

Preparing for a night away from base camp

The language of literary non-fiction

The style of the diary Class and Individual work
One of the things which is striking about this diary is the way in which different entries are written.

■ Suggest some words to help you describe the style of the diary. For example, matter of fact, detailed.

Investigating style Individual work
■ On your own, choose a short quotation to illustrate two or three of these different styles of writing.

■ Write out the quotations and annotate them to show what you notice about the way each one is written. Make sure you consider the following:
- the styles of writing
- the purpose
- the effect on the reader.

The example below shows you the sort of thing you should comment on.

Note form

'today, lunch, we are 21 miles from the depot.
Ill-fortune presses, but better may come.'

words that are no longer commonly used suggests the period this was written in

2nd half of sentence contrasts with the first — optimism — attempt to look on the bright side

Sharing your ideas Group work
■ In small groups, take it in turns to read out and talk about your choices. As a group, decide on three quotations to share with the rest of the class.

Presenting your ideas Class work
■ Listen to each group present their three quotations and agree which category you would put each quotation into:

Poetic
Factual notes
Recount
Description
Other (e.g. personal)

■   Talk about how you decided on the most suitable category for each quotation.

■   Choose one of the quotations from each category and look in more detail at the way it is written. What do you notice? Were there any particular language features which helped you decide which category to place it in? For each category, think about:
- the most frequently used words
- which words are missed out
- the length and type of sentence
- the way the words are arranged in the sentence.

Writing about language   Homework
■   Have a go at doing the same thing for one or two more quotations. Write up your analysis in full sentences.

A history book account

Scott's diary means that anyone writing historical material about his expedition has plenty of information to work with. You are going to use the diary as the basis of a history book account for Year 6 pupils.

What are information books like?   Class and pair work
■   List everything you will need to think about when writing an information book for this age group. Use the ideas suggested here to get you started:
- easy to read
- attractive to look at.

Investigating information books
■   Your teacher will bring in a selection of information books for you to look through. Browse through the books. Make a note of anything which strikes you as a good way of presenting information.

■   What do you think makes a successful information book? Decide on the three most important criteria and suggest these in class discussion.

Sharing what you have learned as whole class

■   Agree on your class criteria for judging information books.

■   Look back at the notes you made on Scott's style of writing. Talk about the changes you will need to make to the way the information is presented and to the style of the diary.

Reading for information   Homework

■   Re-read a photocopy of the extract from Scott's diary. As you read, highlight:
-    the main pieces of information
-    anything you think might appeal to a Year 6 pupil.

Researching a history book

Planning your research   Class work

■   Share your homework and decide on the headings you are going to use to help you research and organise your account of Captain Scott.

Carrying out your research   Individual and pair work

Although the extract from Scott's diary paints a clear picture of what it was like to struggle through the Antarctic, it does not tell you any of the background information you would need to include in a school text book. You will need to do some additional research in the library or on the Internet.

■   Use the following prompts to help you organise your research.

-    Use the headings you have decided on to help you organise your reading and note-making.
-    When you come across a useful book or website, make a note of the title and the author or editor.
-    Use the index or contents page to help you find the pages most relevant to the project. If you are using the Internet, remember to use the search option.
-    Scan the page or chapter to find the sections which look most promising. After you have skim-read the page to check it is going to be useful, you need to read it in more detail. If you are using a book, you might find it helpful to stick post-it notes near the section you want to use. You can use these to jot down any questions or ideas you have, as you go along. If you are using a website, you could copy and paste the most useful and interesting sections into a Word file.
-    Even when you come across a really interesting or useful section of the book there is no need to write down everything. You should only write down the most important words. To help you decide which these are, look back at the quotations from Scott's diary grouped under 'Factual'. Which words have been left out? Which words do you have to keep for the diary to make any sense?

Sharing information   Class work

■   Take it in turns to feed back a useful or interesting piece of information. Make sure you explain how you discovered this, and how you think you might use it in your information book.

Writing the information book

The layout and organisation of information books   Class and individual work

■   Look at the examples your teacher brought in to give you some ideas about how you might present the information.

■   Brainstorm some ways you might present the information you have researched. Remember to check the class criteria for what makes a good information text book.

Writing a first draft

■   Begin by making a sketch of your double page spread. This should include:
-   the headings
-   places for pictures, cartoons, quotations
-   'fact' boxes
-   spaces for longer explanations.

■   Write a first draft, thinking about the purpose and audience.

Getting feedback

■   With a partner, check your first draft against the class criteria.

Presenting your work

■   Take it in turns to present your information book to the class.

■   Sum up what you have learned in this unit about the difference between literary non-fiction and information books. You could think about the following:
-   layout and presentation
-   content
-   tone
-   relationship with the reader.

Did you see...?

Reviews are written about all kinds of products and texts – music, television, films, computer games, plays and books. Reviews play an important role in the broadcasting, publishing, film, computer and music industries. They offer us judgements and guides to all aspects of our cultural life.

> **In this unit you will learn:**
> - about how review writing works as a genre
> - how the content and style of a review is affected by its subject and audience
> - ways of using metaphors and similes in non-fiction writing
> - how to tell the difference between facts and opinions in a review
> - how to evaluate whether a review is effective
> - how to plan, write and evaluate your own review.

Bart Simpson's advice on writing a book review

Reviewing books   Pair and class work
One kind of writing you have probably been asked to do a lot is book reviewing.

- Think back over the book reviews you've done and make brief notes about writing a review.

Whole class discussion
- Talk about your thoughts and feelings when asked to write a review. For example, do you find it easy? Do you know how to present and organise your ideas? Are you confident about using the language of reviews and getting the balance right between fact and opinion?

Bart Simpson's Book Review   Group and class work
- Read *How To Do a Book Report* by Bart Simpson on pages 47 and 48. Make sure you read it closely, including all the annotations. Talk about your reaction to it.

- Try turning Bart's tips into a list of points for each of the following categories: Audience, Purpose, Form.

Sharing your ideas
- Listen to the comments and observations from different groups. Humour is often based upon a kind of truth. What particular truths are exposed in Bart Simpson's guide?

Writing to analyse, review and comment

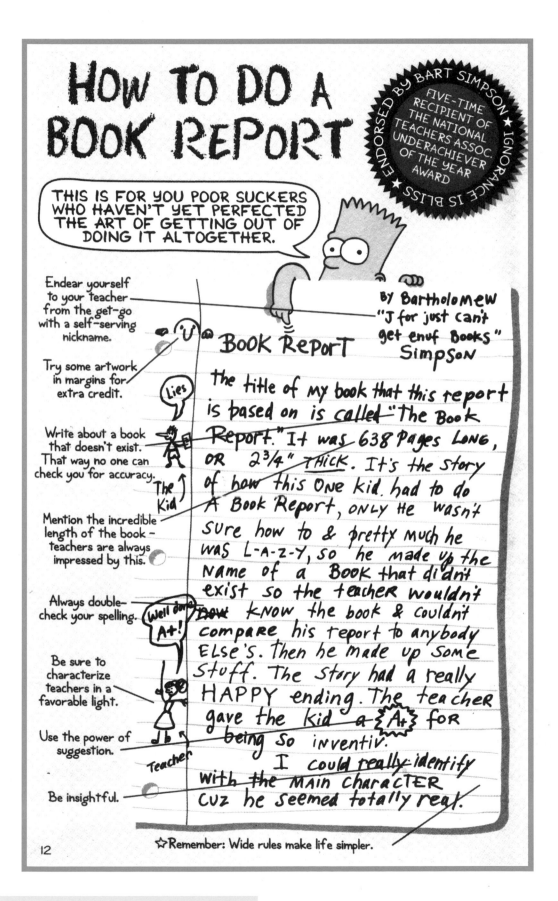

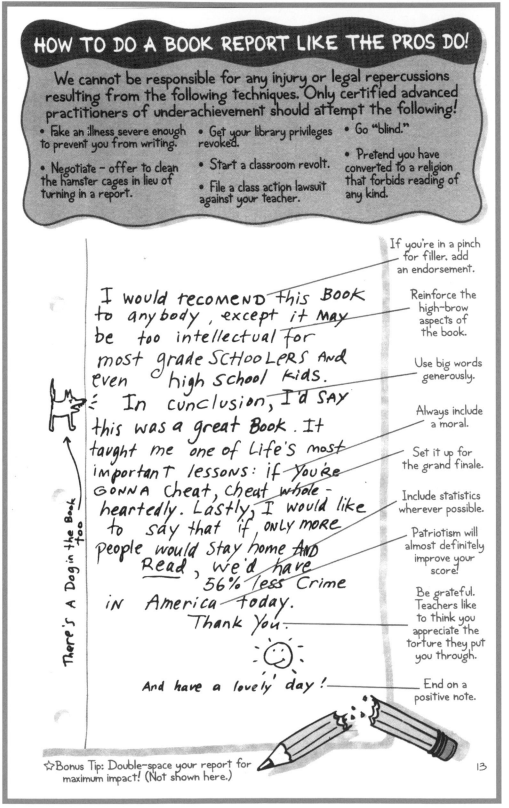

From *Bart Simpson's Guide to Life*

Writing to analyse, review and comment

Investigating review writing

A quick recap Class and pair work

■ Remind yourselves of what you already know about review writing (for example, what they are written for, who reads them, the style of writing typical of reviews and so on).

Some features of review writing Pair work

■ There are five reviews printed on pages 50 and 51.
   Take responsibility for looking in detail at one review. Read your review out loud, looking closely at the language and layout. Pick out of the following features of review writing which are true of the review you are looking at.

Words:
lots of adjectives
lots of nouns
jokes, puns, wordplay
lots of specialist vocabulary.

Sentences:
are written in the present tense
are written in an informal tone
use rhetorical questions to grab the reader's attention
leave out verbs to make an impact.

The whole text:
uses bold print and headlines
includes a visual image
is short (usually between 200 and 800 words)
is often written in columns
has a clear idea of who the audience is
contains personal opinion
refers to other products/texts
includes facts about the product/text
summarises the text
analyses the product/text
offers an evaluation or rating.

Soft toys with hard centres

Fur Fighters

Sega Dreamcast £39.99

Bizarre/Acclaim ★★★☆☆

This is more Quack than Quake, but Fur Fighters solves the problem of gore in third person shooters: you just have to knock the stuffing out of your opponents.

The idea behind Bizarre Creations' game is simple enough: put serious fire power in the hands of some furry toys. This is carried through in Rayman-like 3D cartoon graphics and punning humour. The more difficult aspect of the game is that you have to play all six characters – Roofus the hound, Bungalow the Kangaroo etc – choosing the correct one for the task in hand. It's all a bit tricksy.

But this isn't just a shooter. It's also a 3D action/adventure game, and you have to solve lots of puzzles to get around the six game zones. Some of them are complicated, so finishing the game could take a long time.

The worst thing about the game is the opening 'training' sequence, which also fills in the back story. It goes on far too long. The best thing is the split-screen Fluff Match which provides an arena where you can go fur-to-fur with a friend.

Jack Schofield,
The Guardian, 20th July 2000

Last Night's TV

The Dream Academy (BBC1) followed four students of the Italia conti theatre school ('Very, very gently this afternoon we start humming.'). Ben has a fine voice and can command a loyal coachload of Sunderland supporters when he appears in the West End. Tim is the back end of a cow in Wolverhampton ('I wanted the front end but they said no.'). Kelli knows it cheers you up to kick critics who did not like *Othello*, the musical ('I just wanted to say, "Did you actually watch the show?''. And Georgia, my favourite, could go on as an Essex Eyeore without rehearsal ('I work on a Sunday at B and Q and I can't stand it ... Blokes come and ask you how to fit loft insulation.') She was, much to her surprise, chosen to give a belting rendition of 'Oom pah pah' from Oliver – in St. Paul's of all places. 'Thank God it's over,' groaned Georgia, as heartfelt a prayer as ever Paul's heard.

Nancy Banks Smith,
The Guardian,
5th October 2000

Clockwork or All Wound Up

★★★★★

Philip Pullman, ill Peter Bailey, Doubleday, 96pp, 0 385 40755 6 £9.99 hbk

On a cold winter's night, an apprentice clockmaker, having failed his commission, scowls in a corner of the tavern, as the local storyteller begins his tale, not knowing how it will end. Meanwhile, the master mechanic Dr Kalmenius, sinister genius of the story, strides towards the tavern, dragging an evil gift for the apprentice behind him. Elsewhere, a lost, fictional, clockwork child is also seeking the warmth of the tavern. As 'fiction' and 'fact' engage like cogs, the metamechanic Philip Pullman looks on, making wise little notes in the margin.

Don't miss this book. It's a fascinating meditation on the intricate machinations of narrative, and at the same time a funny, frightening and very moving story.

GH, *Books for Keeps*, March 1997

Eiffel 65 Europop

According to last year's *Smash Hits* poll *Blue* (*Da ba dee*) was your choice for mashin' it up on the dancefloor last year. *Europop* takes everything that made *Blue* a hit (beeps, squelches, weirdified voices etc) and spreads it over 13 tracks. It should be a shiny, dancey 21st century future-fest, but actually, *Europop* sounds like an '80s album sung by a computer suffering from the millennium bug. And sounding '80s is just *soooo* 1999.

John Hindmarch, *Smash Hits*, 26th January 2000

Archer's flop is compelling stuff

As every critic in the land has noted, Jeffrey Archer's courtroom drama, *The Accused*, is a dreadful play, dreadfully acted, and an astonishing act of sheer gall on the part of its writer and star. It's like watching a three hour car crash – appalling, horrific, but you can't tear your eyes away. Even Archer's harshest critics must concede, that for all its faults, *The Accused* is unmissable. ...

It leaves us agog at the spectacle of a man beyond embarrassment, further exposing himself, committing an unwitting case of public self-combustion ... there probably hasn't been anything like it as a piece of public entertainment, since they electrocuted a sick elephant at Coney Island in 1905. It's grisly, awful and utterly hypnotic.

The Evening Standard

Reporting your findings   Group and class work
- Join up with three other pairs who have looked at different reviews. Listen to each pair reporting back what they noticed about their review. As a group, sum up the key features of reviews and what purpose each one serves.

The features of a review   Homework
- Choose two or three of the features of review writing (page 49). For each one write a sentence explaining the reason why it is a feature of review writing. For example, reviews offer an evaluation or rating because one purpose of a review is to advise the reader about what to see or buy.

Toy Story 2 – looking at a film review in more depth

Whole class discussion
- Take it in turns to read out your sentences explaining the typical features of review writing.

Talking about *Toy Story 2*
You are going to analyse a film review of *Toy Story 2*, written by Roger Clarke for *The Big Issue*.

- Share what you know about the film, *Toy Story 2*. If you have seen the film, you could offer your opinions on it.

***Toy Story 2* – facts and opinions**   Individual and class work
- Look closely at the video cover of *Toy Story 2* and compile a list of facts about the film. Make a second list of opinions on the film.

       Writing to analyse, review and comment

Whole class feedback

■ Feed back your ideas about the film.

■ Think of three different places where you might see or hear a review of a film like *Toy Story 2*.

Reviewing *Toy Story 2* Homework

■ Take one of these places where the film *Toy Story 2* might be reviewed.

■ Write the opening and closing sentences of the review. You are trying to show the ways in which any piece of writing is affected by the audience who will read it.

The *Toy Story 2* review

Before reading the review Pair and class work

■ Listen to a few of the opening and closing sentences of your reviews. Talk about the similarities and differences between them.

Roger Clarke's review of *Toy Story 2* is a challenging read. Before reading the whole text you are going to do some work on key words and phrases from the review.

■ Study the words and phrases carefully. Note down any questions raised for you by any of the words. Use a dictionary or your teacher to check any meanings you are not sure of. Make any links you can see between any of the words and phrases.

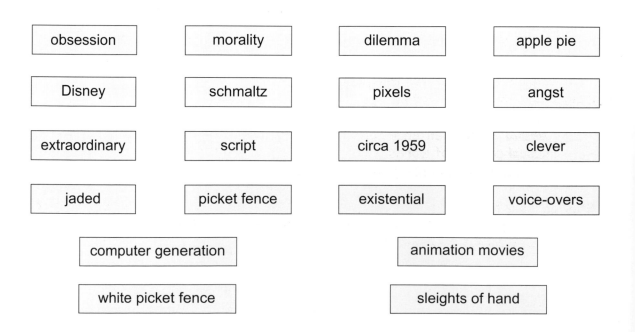

obsession	morality	dilemma	apple pie
Disney	schmaltz	pixels	angst
extraordinary	script	circa 1959	clever
jaded	picket fence	existential	voice-overs
computer generation		animation movies	
white picket fence		sleights of hand	

Writing to analyse, review and comment

Whole class discussion

■ Share some of your ideas and questions. Sort out any words or ideas that you don't understand.

Reading the *Toy Story 2* review

■ Listen to the review being read aloud. As you listen, make brief notes recording your thoughts and questions about the review.

I don't particularly share the general obsession with animation movies: in fact, I pretty much disapprove of a handful of pixels and voiceovers getting the same amount of attention as your more traditional movie. But **Toy Story 2** charmed me. OK, so its purveying a white-picket fence morality circa 1959 (about time we had an animated 'Mom's apple pie' movie with a great Bramley-filled sugar-toasted hero don't you think?) and is honeycombed with pure Disney schmaltz. But *Toy Story 2* provoked shrieks of delight in the audience of kids I saw it with – and for jaded old critics like me, the many sleights of hand (both visually and in the script) provided constant small pops of pleasure. The sight of 'Sticky Pete' – voiceover Kelsey Grammar – chatting up a couple of Barbie dolls (an industry joke about 'Mr Loverman' Grammar if ever there was one) was merely one of a legion of fresh and clever gags.

John Lasseter has actually surpassed the original movie in this one – which has the cowboy Woody (voiceover Tom Hanks) stolen by an evil toy trader who knows he's a rare collectable item. Reunited with other 1950s toys in his original set – a cowgirl Jessie (Joan Cusack) and Stinky Pete the gold prospector – Woody's dilemma is whether to stay with his old family and sit out life in a Japanese museum or return to a regular kid who will play with him.

There's further existential angst when Buzz Lightyear (Tim Allen) visits a toyshop and sees thousands of versions of himself, none of whom realise yet that they are toys. It's fast, clever and often exquisitely beautiful to look at (those turquoise and jade colours in the Lightyear shelving show how much this type of computer generation can do extraordinarily novel things with the medium of light). I loved it ...

■ Skim read the review again. Either annotate a photocopy of the review or make brief notes on the following points:
- the length of the review
- the layout
- the first three sentences and the ending
- unusual choices of words
- the writer's relationship with the reader.

Sharing your responses

■ Talk about what you noticed about this review. How far does it meet your expectations? Does anything surprise you?

A brief summing up Homework

■ Write brief notes summing up what you have learned so far about the way this review is written.

Evaluating the review of *Toy Story 2*

The writer's comments on the review Class work

The reviewer, Roger Clarke, explained his reasons for writing the review in this way. His comments have been organised into word, sentence and text level work.

■ Listen to Roger Clarke's comments on the review being read to you and compare his analysis with your own.

Word

Compound words

I use the word Disney-schmaltz to bring together the ideas of Disney and a sickly sentimentalism. It just means soft-soaping, sugary, too sweet.

Imagery

I use two or three sugar images in that sentence: 'apple pie', 'sugar toasted', 'honeycombed'. And then 'small pops of pleasure' is an unusual image to use to describe an audience reaction but I wanted to include an odd image to get the reader's attention and because there was something quite unusual about the effect on the audience.

Sentence

The first sentence

I started off with a deliberate generalisation. People are going to read that and think 'What and idiot' or they're going to think 'That's interesting.' But whichever they think they're probably going to read on. So you've kind of hooked them because you've made a slightly argumentative point.

The second sentence is

deliberately short after that very long first sentence. It's like the rhythm of speech. I've deliberately contradicted myself and offered an alternative point of view. I'm also trying to

humanise it by saying 'This film changed my mind about animation movies. I went into this film not really expecting enjoy it but I did.' Reviewers have to confront their prejudices all the time.

The third sentence

This begins with 'OK' which is colloquial and friendly – a personal touch. I'm saying that I liked it even though it's putting across the usual old Disney ideas and values about family life and a golden time in the 1950s. It's a really long sentence because it's a sort of breathless summary, the sort someone might make in a conversation to get something explained quickly before moving on and before being interrupted.

Punctuation

I like dashes – they look nice and they help to get a rhythm going. Somehow they're not as serious as a comma or a bracket. They're a sort of quick, informal aside to the reader.

The final sentence

'I loved it' may seem a bit strong but it sums it all up really. The warmth and loveableness of the film. I don't usually come down with such a heavy personal recommendation but this also connects well with the beginning where I said that I wasn't expecting to like this film.

Text

The layout

Generally what a film review has to have in it is the title, the classification (which age it's for) the name of the film director lead actors and some sort of star rating. Because film is a visual medium there is always a still from the film included which in *The Big Issue* only leaves room for about 800 words.

Writer's relationship with the reader

I refer to 'jaded old critics like me' because readers quite like it if you show that you don't think too much of yourself.

The ending

Towards the end of the second paragraph I start to wind it up and start thinking about how to end it. Originally I had more here about the use of light but the editor chopped it out.

Writing to analyse, review and comment

Collecting reviews   Homework

■   Collect some examples of the kind of review you would like to write yourself (for example, a film, book or CD review).

Writing a review

A reviewer should ...   Class work

■   Draw up a set of criteria for writing an effective review. You could do this as a list of what a reviewer should try to do, and the pitfalls a reviewer should try to avoid.

Preparing to write your own review   Individual and pair work

■   Look back at the work you have done in this unit, especially the examples of reviews on pages 50 and 51 and the lists of features on pages 49.

■   Choose what you would like to review – it could be a TV programme, a computer game, film or a new single. Decide where you would like the review to appear (for example, a newspaper, magazine or website).

Researching the content of your review
- Look closely at the reviews you have both brought in. You should think about:
  - the sorts of magazine they were published in
  - the sorts of reader they are talking to
  - the kinds of things these reviews include
  - the balance between opinion and factual information
  - the amount of detail they go into
  - the tone and relationship with the reader.

Researching the audience for your review
- Choose the newspaper or magazine you each plan to write for. It is a good idea to choose one which you are familiar with. Talk about the style, layout and audience it is aimed at and draw up a fact sheet about your audience. Start by telling each other, 'Our typical reader is ... '

Composing key words and sentences
- Talk together about key words and sentences you could use in your individual reviews. Focus on the following:
  - the beginning
  - the ending
  - the way you'll change paragraphs
  - the way you will interest the reader (jokes, references to other one texts or products)
  - the way you'll include a few facts about the text/product.

Sharing good ideas
- Listen to a few of the key words and sentences that different pairs plan to use. Make a note of any of these that you had not thought of. Share your good ideas and try to sort out any difficulties people have.

Writing a review Homework
- Write a review of between 200 and 500 words.

- Compare your draft against the class criteria for writing an effective review. You might also find it helpful to read it to one or two other people and ask for their feedback. Make any changes you think are necessary.

- Write the final version of the review. If you can, use a computer to help you with the layout and presentation.

Writing to analyse, review and comment

Dirty Dogs

In this unit you will learn:
- how to tell others your point of view
- how to examine the structure and language of information and instruction texts
- how to read an opinion column which expresses a point of view
- how to write one of the following:
  - a letter to an MP demanding action
  - a public information leaflet
  - an opinion column for a newspaper.

Getting the facts

Reading an information text   Pair and class work

■ Read *The Independent's* 'Dirty Dogs Campaign' fact sheet. Talk about what you think are the most serious issues raised by the fact sheet.

■ Choose the five facts that you think it is most important to know.

Foul Facts	What can be done?	Underfoot overseas

Foul Facts

❑There are 7.5 million dogs in Britain, producing 1,000 tonnes of faeces a day.

❑There is no national legislation – only by-laws – to compel owners to clean up after their dogs.

❑The maximum fine is £500. The maximum for litter is £2,500 (£1,000 in Northern Ireland).

❑Toxocara canis is the roundworm carried by puppies, and some adult dogs. The worms are expelled in the faeces. There is no obligation for owners to have dogs "wormed".

❑Toxocariasis disease can cause asthma, epilepsy and blindness, but also milder symptoms such as fevers and coughs. More than 200 cases are reported every year, mostly in children. Around eight children a month develop eye disease as a result of Toxocara infection.

❑Toxocariasis can be caught by swallowing soil contaminated by Toxocara eggs. The eggs can survive in soil for two or three years. They cannot be destroyed with disinfectant.

❑It takes two weeks for faeces to become infectious. Fresh faeces pose no threat from Toxocara, "Poop-scooping" is therefore safe and effective.

❑Soil surveys of London parks have found two-thirds contaminated with Toxocara eggs.

What can be done?

DIRTY DOGS CAMPAIGN

❑The issue on which MPs receive most complaints is dog fouling.

❑"Poop scoops" are provided free by some local authorities; pet shops sell them for around £3 for 20. Old plastic bags and bits of cardboard do equally well.

Wanted: a solution that can work

USA: On the spot fines up to $100 in some cities. Pavements "pretty clean".

Belgium: 1.2 million dogs. Voluntary registration. "Worse than London, disgusting."

France: 9.5 million dogs. Compulsory registration. Fouling fines imposed by traffic

Underfoot overseas

wardens. Parisian clean-up operation using 100 motorised pooper scoopers or "caninettes" costs £4 million annually. Pavements "not too bad".

Germany: 3.6 million dogs. Dog tax around £30. Leash laws; some park areas set aside for dogs. Pavements "dreadful".

Iceland: Dogs banned from Reykjavik and other urban centres until mid 1980s because of worm problems. Now allowed into town: maximum £20 fine for fouling.

Ireland: 600,000 dogs. National licensing. Dog free zones in parks. Pavements "better than in England".

Italy: 5.5 million dogs. Compulsory registration. "Dogs foul roads and pavements; whatever the laws are they are not enforced."

Netherlands: 1.8 million dogs. Voluntary registration. No fouling legislation; "the streets of Amsterdam are not clean".

Spain: 3 million dogs. Registration and licensing scheme. Pavements "not that clean".

Sweden: 700,000 dogs. Stockholm has leash laws, poop scoop schemes and dog-free zones. Streets "perfectly clear. Very little mess of any kind".

A public information leaflet

Shared reading   Group and individual work

Scoop the Poop on pages 63 and 64 is an example of a different sort of information leaflet. It has been produced by the Pet Advisory Committee. It gives information about dog fouling and advice on how to deal with the problem. It is also intended to persuade people to behave in a particular way.

■   Read the leaflet out loud, sharing the reading between you. As you read, make a note of anything that you notice about this text and the ways in which it is typical of information texts.

A list of features

■   In the chart below is a list of features that you might have noticed. See if you can find an example of some of these and say why you think each has been used.

Layout	Vocabulary	Sentence	The whole text
illustrations and diagrams	a serious objective tone	use of the present tense	a clear introduction and conclusion
text which is broken up into chunks	the use of specialist nouns	use of simple, short sentences	a sequential argument
a balance between the text and illustrations	the use of rhyme and wordplay.	imperative verbs giving instructions	dominated by factual information
use of bullet points to make instructions clear.		varying the length of sentences for impact	a third person voice
		the use of the conditional conjunction 'if'	often addressed to 'you' (second person).
		the use of questions as headings.	

Writing to inform, persuade and argue

Does the leaflet succeed? Class work

■   Talk about how well you think this leaflet succeeds in its purpose which is:
-   to inform people of the problem of dog fouling
-   be extremely clear
-   reach a wide audience
-   persuade people to 'scoop the poop'.

Thinking about argument Homework

■   Jot down everything you know about arguments. You could do this as a spider diagram with lines connecting your different ideas.

■   What are the similarities and differences between texts which inform, argue and persuade? Think of the *Scoop the Poop* leaflet and the way it combines information and argument in order to persuade people to 'scoop the poop'.

Column 1

Column 2

Column 3

A cleaner neighbourhood. We all want it. We can all help to achieve it.

No one likes dog mess. This leaflet explains how you – as a responsible dog owner – can do your bit by helping reduce dog mess on the streets, parks and beaches.

The importance of training

Being a responsible dog owner means more than making sure your dog is fed and looked after. Dogs need to be trained and part of this is toilet training.

It is best to train when the dog is still a puppy. But older dogs can learn too.

How to start: A puppy goes to the toilet very frequently, so begin by putting him outside in a suitable spot if you think he seems to want to go. Keep repeating this and praise him when he finishes. If you can't get outside, get your puppy to use a litter tray.

Regular times: get your dog used to a routine. Build up regular times when you take him out – in the morning, after a meal and at night.

Going on command: Use a command word such as 'clean' or 'busy' just as he is about to go to the toilet. Always use the same tone of voice and praise him when he has finished. Training him means he will go where you want him to – and not in unsuitable places.

Going at home

If you've got a garden, then why not screen off a small area where you can train your dog to go. You can then bury the mess in the garden or pick it up using a poop scoop. Your Council should tell you if they have special arrangements for disposal of poop scoops. Otherwise wrap up your used poop scoop in a plastic bag and dispose of it with your normal household waste.

If you don't have a garden and your dog is not too large, try training your dog to use a litter tray. Dispose of the contents of the litter tray by double wrapping it in plastic bags and dispose of it with your normal household waste.

But what when I am out with my dog?

If your dog needs to go while you're out, 'scoop the poop'. You can buy all sorts of different poop scoops cheaply at pet shops and some supermarkets. Some local councils have their own poop scoops which are available from council offices or from vending

machines. If you don't have a poop scoop with you, you can use a newspaper or plastic bag.

If you use a poop scoop, you will not need to touch the mess directly, many designs of poop scoop involve a plastic bag which can be tied up before you dispose of it.

Remember to wash your hands as soon as you can afterwards.

Dog mess can contain a number of things which can make people ill – best known of which is toxocara canis, which is a roundworm. If the eggs of the worm are swallowed this can result in a range of symptoms from aches and pains to bronchial conditions. In rare cases, eye sight can be damaged.

The risk to human health is small. You can reduce it further by:
● worming your dog regularly
● always cleaning up after your dog
● good hygiene practice.

What should I do with the poop scoop when it's been used?

Many councils provide special bins where you can put your used poop scoops. Dog waste bins are often red.

If there are no bins around, take the poop scoop home and dispose of it. If that is not possible, then as a last resort wrap the used poop scoop again in a plastic bag and dispose of it in a litter bin.

Inside of leaflet

Column 4

Worms can affect a dog at any age. Caring for your dog therefore includes making sure your dog is wormed regularly.

Worms cause sickness and diarrhoea in young animals but adult dogs may show no symptoms. Worming is easy, effective and costs very little. You can get worming tablets from your pharmacist, vet, pet shop or larger branches of supermarkets. Follow the maker's instructions carefully. The treatment required depends on your dog's weight.

Adult dogs should be wormed at least every 6 months. Pregnant dogs and bitches with young puppies should be wormed more frequently. With puppies seek veterinary advice, but in general puppies should be wormed when they are about 2 weeks old and then treated at regular intervals until they are 6 months old.

Column 5

Poop scooping and the law

Local councils (and some other organisations like water companies and the British Waterways Board) can make local laws, called bye-laws. These can require you to clean up after your dog in designated areas, such as streets, parks and beaches.

Do not wait until the law makes you clear up. It is in everyone's interest that dog mess is not left lying where people might tread or sit in it.

You can do your bit.
Scoop the Poop – Clear up after your dog.

Further help and advice on aspects of responsible pet ownership.

Pet Advisory Committee
1 Dean's Yard, London, SW1P 3NR

This leaflet is produced by the
Department of the Environment
in association with the Pet Advisory Committee

Front page

SCOOP THE POOP!

Clear up after your dog

Department of the Environment
Welsh Office

Cover of Leaflet

Putting forward an opinion

You and argument   Pair and class work

■   Talk about the role argument plays in your life. Use the questions to focus your discussion.

- What do you understand by the word 'argument'?
- What are the different ways that you listen to, or take part in 'argument' ? (For example, at home or at school; in the street; in things that you read in comics, magazines and newspapers and in what you watch on television.)
- What are your feelings about having arguments with other people?
- What do you think are your strengths and weaknesses in presenting your point of view in speaking and in writing?
- When might it be useful to be able to represent a point of view other than your own?

Writing to inform, persuade and argue

Information or argument?

■ Talk about the differences between information and argument texts. Use the *Scoop the Poop* article to collect together some of the features and phrases which you associate with the two different sorts of non-fiction text.

■ Take it in turns to feed back your ideas.

The local council have called a public meeting to discuss the problem of dog mess and the *Dogs (Fouling of Land) Act 1996*. Your teacher will play the role of the local councillor who has called the meeting. Five people will be given one of the role cards. The rest of the class will be told whether they are on the side of the supporters of the *Dogs (Fouling of Land) Act 1996* or not.

Preparing your point of view

■ Make brief notes on the arguments you want to put forward in role.

Public meeting role play   Group and class work

■ Use what you have learned so far to take part in a role play debating the issues.

Deciding on a plan of action

■ Recap the arguments expressed during the meeting and list the possible actions that could be recommended to the council.

Report back your ideas

■ Take it in turns to report back your ideas and agree a plan of action.

Dirty Dogs Public Meeting Role Cards

A

You love dogs and think that dogs play an important part in the happiness of people. You regularly walk your dog in the park. You think the whole argument about dog mess has got out of hand. The idea of dog owners having to pick up their dogs' mess is ridiculous to you. You think that dog mess is completely natural and people should learn to live with it; it's washed away by the rain and is completely bio-degradeable. If everyone was taught to wash their hands before they ate, as your family do, then there would be no problem.

B

You own a small dog who travels to work with you in the car everyday so that he doesn't get lonely at home. The journey is quite long but there's a small park next to your office. This is a convenient place for him relieve himself. So twice a day you stop at the park gates and let him out. It's easy for you because you don't have to park properly or get out of the car. Sometimes you get angry comments from people, especially if they've got small children, but you tell them it's a free country and you'd like to know where else your dog is supposed to relieve himself.

C

You got fed up with the habit of one dog in your neighbourhood who always used your front gate to defecate. In an attempt to do something about it you have organised a Tidy Up Our Street Campaign. You leafleted local homes about the problem and talked to the owner of the dog that always uses your front gate as its toilet. You've persuaded the council to put notices on lamposts reminding dog owners that if their dog fouls the pavements they are liable for a £500 fine. Recently you have received hate mail and had dog excrement left at your front door.

D

You are the parent of two small children and you often have to clean dog mess off their shoes, hands and the wheels of the buggy. Every time you take your children to the park you feel angry about the way that dog owners disobey the byelaws about keeping dogs on leads and keeping dogs out of the children's play area. You sometimes feel that always having to be on the lookout for dog mess makes playing in the park a miserable experience for you and your children. You also worry about the health risks to your children but don't really know much about them.

E

You are a London doctor who has carried out research into Toxocara and identified 'a significant health risk'. You know that all puppies have worms and that soil surveys of London parks have found two thirds are contaminated with Toxocara eggs. You know that symptoms of toxocariasis include fever, abdominal pain, rashes, anaemia and general 'failure to thrive'. You are also aware that toxocariasis disease can cause asthma, epilepsy and blindness as well as coughs. You feel the health risk should be taken much more seriously, especially as the eggs survive in the soil for two or three years. Poop scoops seem to you the only answer if this hazard is to be removed from parks.

A personal opinion – reading a newspaper column

Although *Scoop the Poop* is written in a very reasonable, clear tone, dog mess is a subject about which some people can get quite angry and which others find quite funny. The text on page 68 is from a weekly newspaper column – a short regular slot in a national paper where the writer airs his or her views. Newspaper columns are often examples of more extreme personal viewpoints.

What do you notice about this text?   Class and pair work
- Discuss your first reactions to this piece of writing about dog mess. Use the questions suggested here to focus your ideas.

- What tone of voice does the writer adopt?
- Is she being completely serious?
- What do you think is the aim of this piece of writing?

Analysing 'Home Thoughts'
Like many non-fiction texts, this text crosses the boundaries of several non-fiction types. Sometimes its purpose is to entertain, sometimes to argue and sometimes to persuade. Some of the techniques used in this text are listed on page 69.

- Find examples of each technique and note them down.

- Take it in turns to feed back your observations and analysis.

The author on writing techniques   Class viewing
- Listen to Justine Picardie talk about the techniques she used in this piece to get her message across

Summing up the differences
- Finally, draw up a list of the main differences that you can identify between this text and *Scoop the Poop*.

A short comparison   Homework
- Write one or two paragraphs comparing the two types of writing: the opinion column and the information leaflet. Use the phrases suggested here to help you structure the comparison.

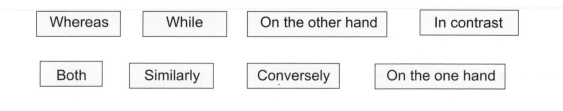

| Whereas | While | On the other hand | In contrast |

| Both | Similarly | Conversely | On the one hand |

If I ruled the world, which is of course unlikely, I would ban dogs from cities. This is something I have been thinking a lot about recently: not the world-rule bit but the dogs. Perhaps I'm obsessional, but dog mess is everywhere these days. More and more of it. My son tramples through it blithely on the pavements and in the park and then runs into the house, and I clear it up, muttering dark threats against all dog owners.

I used to think lonely old people should be allowed to keep dogs but I've hardened my views. Apart from guide dogs for the blind, they've all got to go. The old people will have to content themselves with hamsters or goldfish, or perhaps a fluffy rabbit. (I'm not too keen on cats, since the neighbour's one started defecating in my pot of tulip bulbs, killing them all stone dead.)

In my more enraged Mussolini-like moments, I think dogs should be banned from the countryside, too, except for useful creatures such as sheep-dogs. I went for a bracing walk in Lynmouth two weeks ago, and there they were, evil little heaps of excrement just waiting to be trodden in: next to a waterfall along the sea front, in the woods. Imagine if we let our children pull down their knickers and poo everywhere, completely at will. Imagine the outrage.

And another thing. Our local park has one small fenced patch – a children's playground – where dogs are banned (though that doesn't stop them leaping over the fence and infesting the sandpit with Toxocariasis, while their owners look on benignly). The rest of the park – the muddy expanses of grass, the bleak flower beds, the tragic little rose garden – is dominated by dogs. Great big slavering

dogs, small yappy dogs, all chasing children, scaring babies, and shitting everywhere. You can't have a picnic in the summer without inspecting the grass first, or play football without falling over in some fetid heap. What is this about dogs and their owners that makes them so much more important than anyone else?

I'm not mad enough to suggest compulsory dog euthanasia, but once the ban is enforced I'm afraid all dogs will have to be sterilized. And despite the cries of outrage that would ensue, there would be very large fines for dog-owners who allow their animals to foul the streets or parks, without clearing it up immediately. The fines would be like parking tickets: issued by zealots, no argument, just pay up. The money raised could be spent by local authorities on those snazzy municipal street-cleaning machines – the ones like giant Hoovers, with washing bits attached.

Then we could all walk along with our heads held high, enjoying the beauties of nature and our fellow men, instead of being forced to watch our every step because of the stinking perils that lie beneath our feet. And the world would be a much happier place. Simple really –.

Justine Picardie, *The Independent on Sunday*, 16th January 1994

Techniques	Effect on the reader
Grammar use of commas and dashes as parenthesis	**Grammar** establishes informal relationship with reader
colon used	to introduce a list
use of first person	emphasises personal opinion of writer
varying sentence lengths	adds impact and rhythm
similar to spoken English	intimate, friendly style
sentences without verbs	breaking the rules emphasises informal style and independence of the writer
Persuasive techniques use of example and evidence	**Persuasive techniques** short, snappy, entertaining
rhetorical questions	persuades the reader to agree with writer
deliberately extreme standpoint	emphasises the writer's strong feelings
Vocabulary compound words	**Vocabulary** catchy, memorable,
use of slang and taboo words	funny informal relationship with reader, shock to show strong feelings
specialist vocabulary	shows knowledge, serious research
exaggeration	humour, gets attention

Writing a letter to your MP

Oona King addressing Parliament

■　You are going to write a letter to your MP explaining your views on dog mess. What kind of tone will you need to use?

■　Jot down a few key requirements of such a letter, starting with the ones suggested here.

It will need to be quite formal.
It will need to be expressed in a reasonable tone.

The language of argument and persuasion　Pair work
You've had some practice in spoken argument and persuasion – writing it down effectively is quite difficult. The words and phrases listed on page 71 are all used by people trying to express their opinions either in conversation or in writing.

■　Sort the phrases into two columns: 'Spoken argument' and 'Written argument'. You might find that some phrases fit into both columns.

■　Choose one phrase from each column to help you express the following:
-　your view
-　your view with some exceptions
-　further points to back up your point of view
-　disagreement with another argument
-　recognition of someone else's views
-　your conclusion.

Writing to inform, persuade and argue

Consider the alternatives

There are those who would say that

Don't give me that

On the other hand

I don't go along with that

In addition

At the end of the day

A further point

There are people that think that

Although

But what you haven't thought about is

However

Moreover

Some people believe that

What you're saying is

And another thing

You've got to look at it from my point of view

In conclusion

Yes but

On the one hand

Rubbish

I accept that

No but

Let me sum up by saying

Yet

An alternative point of view would claim that

I believe

On the contrary

What's more

If you get my meaning

Nevertheless

On the one hand

After all is said and done

I think

But

I realise, but

This is what I think

It's my opinion that

Finally

You've got to balance it with this

Do you get my drift?

With respect

You cannot be serious!

It is the case that

On the whole, I agree

Beginning to draft your piece

■ Make a list of the main points you want to make in your piece. Use the information and opinion texts you have read and your work in class discussion to help you.

■ Put your points into rank order, starting with the most important. Experiment with a few ways of linking the paragraphs together.

The writing frame below suggests one way of structuring the letter.

■ Annotate and alter a photocopy of the writing frame with your ideas about how you could use it to structure and develop your notes.

Shared writing   Group work

■ Take it in turns to go through your outline for the letter. Share any difficulties you had and talk about possible ways of overcoming these problems.

■ Use your individual ideas to write a class letter. Focus on the key parts of any argument:
- the first paragraph
- the conclusion
- the first sentence of each paragraph (the topic sentence)
- different ways you could connect the ideas and lead your reader through your argument.

■ Talk about why some suggestions are more effective than others.

Writing your letter   Homework

■ Redraft the letter to your MP.

Your address and MP's address

Paragraph 1: Opening statement
How are you going to begin this letter and let the reader know what it's going to be about and what to expect from it?

Paragraph 2: First point and elaboration
What is the most important thing you want to say in support of legislation against dog mess. How will you develop the point in a way that will convince the reader it is important?

Paragraph 3: Second point and elaboration

Paragraph 4: Third point and elaboration

Paragraph 5: Take account of the opposite point of view and summarise the opening statement
How will you end the letter in a way that shows you have thought fully about the topic and the views of others who may not agree with you? What would be the most effective final sentence? It should both link back to the beginning and leave the reader with something memorable to think about.

Writing to inform, persuade and argue

Letter to Daniel

> **In this unit you will:**
> - read an example of a literary non-fiction text which uses many of the techniques of fiction
> - have a chance to write a piece of literary non-fiction using some of these techniques
> - explore the ways a piece of personal writing can also have a wider significance
> - learn how to write a more formal critical essay
> - learn how to compare texts and to consider different readers' responses to texts.

What sort of writing is this?

Fiction or non-fiction? Class and pair work

- The words listed below have all been used by people trying to explain the differences between fiction and non-fiction.

- Try putting these words into three different groups, under the headings 'Fiction', 'Non-fiction' and 'Both/Not sure'. Talk about how you made your decisions and any differences of opinion.

| personal | imaginative | creative | tells a story |

| for an unknown reader | found mainly in print texts |

| found on TV or radio | deals with facts | deals with ideas |

| about real people | about made up characters |

| hard to read | enjoyable to read |

Exploring the opening of a text
- The first paragraph of the text you are going to read has been broken into fragments. Look closely at the fragments and make notes about your ideas, expectations and questions, for example who is it about? What is happening? When? Where?

> Behind the bedroom door you are sleeping

> I can hear your snores rattling down the stairs

> to our ruined sitting room

> here among the broken chairs,

> the overturned Christmas tree,

> we are preparing to leave you.

> We are breaking away from you, Da.

Sharing your ideas

■ Take it in turns to feed back your ideas to the rest of the class. Make a note of any new ideas which you find interesting.

'Letter to my Father'   Class work

The title of this piece is: 'Letter to my Father'. Immediately underneath the title is the heading:

> Cork, December 1995
> Eamon Patrick Keane died on 5 January 1990

■ Talk about how the title and heading help develop your ideas about the piece.

Listening to the letter

■ Now listen to the whole letter being read out loud.

Responding to the letter   Individual and pair work

■ When you have heard the whole letter, make a note of the impact it has on you.

■ Jot down one or two phrases or sentences from the piece that you find especially powerful or moving.

Writing about your response   Homework

■ Write one or two paragraphs explaining your personal response to the letter. You should think about the content of the letter and the way in which Fergal Keane describes his memories and expresses his feelings.

Letter to my father

Cork, December 1995
Eamon Patrick Keane died on 5 January 1990

Behind the bedroom door you are sleeping. I can hear your snores rattling down the stairs to our ruined sitting-room. Here among the broken chairs, the overturned Christmas tree, we are preparing to leave you. We are breaking away from you, Da.

Last night you crashed through the silence, dead drunk and spinning in your own wild orbit into another year of dreams. This would be the year of the big break – of Hollywood, you said. Oh, my actor father, time was, time was we swallowed those lines, but no longer.

Before leaving I look into the bedroom to where your hand droops out from under the covers, below it the small empty Power's bottle, and I say goodbye. And at seven o'clock on New Year's day we push the old Ford Anglia down the driveway, my mother, brother and I. We push because the engine might wake you, and none of us can face a farewell scene. I don't know what the neighbours think, if anything, when they see a woman and two small boys stealing away in the grey morning, but I don't care, we're heading south with everything we own.

The day I turned twelve, which was four days later, you called to say happy birthday. You were, as I remember, halfway sober, but you didn't say much else, except to ask for my mother who would not come to the phone.

In the background I could hear glasses clinking, voices raised, and you said: 'Tell her I love her,' and then the change ran out, and I began to understand what made love the saddest word in any language.

Christmas that year you had access to the children. We met in Cork station. I remember your new suit, your embarrassed embrace, the money you pressed into our hands, and the smell of whiskey. We found a taxi and the driver stared after us, throwing his eyes to heaven and shaking his head.

What I see now are many such faces: the waitress at the Old Bridge Café where drinks were spilled; the couple who asked for an autograph and watched your shaking hand struggle to write, before they beat a mortified retreat. And on through pubs and bookmakers' shops to one last café where Elvis was crooning 'Love Me Tender, Love Me Sweet' on an ancient radio. By now, nobody was able to speak.

There was a taxi ride home, we children in the back, you in the front, and what lives with me still, always, is the moment of leave-taking, Christmas 1972. Because as the car drove you away from our lives, I saw through steamed-up windows that your eyes had become waterfalls.

I was too young to understand what you knew – that we were lost to you, broken away. Down the years we struggled to find one another, but I was growing up and away, and you were drifting closer to darkness. And at the end I gave up writing, gave up calling. I gave up. Until one night my cousin called to say you were gone. It was a few days into the New Year, and your heart simply gave up in a small room in the town in north Kerry where you were born. I remember that you sent me the collected stories of Raymond Carver for Christmas. I had sent you nothing, not even a card. Now I would send you a thousand, but I have no address.

Writing about the past

What do you know about recounts?   Pair and class work
Fergal Keane's letter is a form of recount – it tells the reader about events in his past life.

■   What tense do you expect recounts to be written in, the past or present?

Exploring the structure

■   Skim through the text and find one place where Fergal Keane changes tense. Talk about the reasons you think he shifted tense at this point.

■   Share your ideas with the rest of the class. What is the effect of writing about a memory in this way?

■   The final sentence is re-printed for you here. What do you think it means?

> 'I had sent you nothing, not even a card. Now I would send you a thousand, but I have no address.'

■   How does Fergal Keane prepare the reader for the final sentence? Look back through the letter and talk about whether it alters your response to what you have read.

A personal recount – experimenting with ways of telling   Individual and pair work
■   Look back at the notes you made on your memories. Choose one memory to write about in more detail.

■   Write a paragraph in the present tense, describing the incident as though it is happening now. Look back at paragraphs one, three and seven of 'Letter to my Father' to help you see how to do this.

■   Write a second paragraph in the past tense, from the point of view of your older self looking back and commenting on why this incident is so important to you.

■   Experiment with a few different endings to your recount.

■   Read your recount to another person in the class and annotate it with any comments or suggestions they have.

Ways of writing powerfully   Class and individual work
■   Share what you have learned about ways of making recount writing interesting and powerful. Some things you might have experimented with include: the length of sentences, tenses, word choices and poetic techniques such as alliteration.

■   Re-draft your personal recount in the light of the feed back you received from the reader in your class

A Letter to Daniel

Investigating vocabulary   Class and pair work

'Letter to my Father' is the first letter in a best-selling collection called *Letter to Daniel: Despatches from the Heart*. Daniel is the writer's baby son. The writer of the piece itself is Fergal Keane, a journalist who has done television, radio and newspaper reports from all over the world.

■ Use the questions suggested here to help you think about the title of the collection.

– What does the word 'Despatches' mean?
– When would you normally expect to use this word?
– Where are despatches usually from?
– Why is the colon used?

■ Brainstorm what you expect from this letter, given what you already know about 'Letter to my Father' and the title of the whole collection.

Reading 'Letter to Daniel'

■ Listen to the whole letter being read out loud, without making any notes.

First responses

■ In pairs, spend a few minutes talking about, and noting down your responses. You might choose to do this as notes or full sentences or visual images. What sticks in your mind?

■ Join up with another pair and share your responses.

Letter to Daniel

Hong Kong, February 1996
Daniel Patrick Keane was born on 4 February, 1996

My dear son, it is six o'clock in the morning on the island of Hong Kong. You are asleep cradled in my left arm and I am learning the art of one-handed typing. Your mother, more tired, yet more happy than I've ever known her, is sound asleep in the room next door, and there is a soft quiet in our apartment.

Since you've arrived, days have melted into night and back again and we are learning a new grammar, a long sentence whose punctuation marks are feeding and winding and nappy changing and these occasional moments of quiet.

When you're older we'll tell you that you were born in Britain's last Asian colony in the lunar year of the pig and that when we brought you home, the staff of the apartment block gathered to wish you well. 'It's a boy, so lucky, so lucky. We Chinese love boys,' they told us. One man said you were the first baby to be born in the block in the year of the pig. This he told us, was good Feng Shui, in other words a positive sign for the building and everyone who lived there.

Naturally your mother and I were only too happy to believe that. We had wanted you and waited for you, imagined you and dreamed about you and now that you are here, no dream can do justice to you. Outside the window, below us on the harbour, the ferries are ploughing back and forth to Kowloon. Millions are already up and moving about and the sun is slanting through the tower blocks and out on to the flat silver waters of the South China Sea. I can see the contrail of a jet over Lamma Island and, somewhere out there, the last stars flickering towards the other side of the world.

We have called you Daniel Patrick but I've been told by my Chinese friends that you should have a Chinese name as well and this glorious dawn sky makes me think we'll call you Son of the Eastern Star. So that later when you and I are far from Asia, perhaps standing on a beach some evening, I can point at the sky and tell you of the Orient and the times and the people we knew there in the last years of the twentieth century.

Your coming has turned me upside down and inside out. So much that seemed essential to me has, in the past few days, taken on a different colour. Like many correspondents I know I have lived a life that, on occasion, has veered close to the edge: war zones, natural disasters, darkness in all its shapes and forms.

In a world of insecurity and ambition and ego, it's easy to be drawn in, to take chances with our lives, to believe that what we do and what people say about us is reason enough to gamble with death. Now, looking at your sleeping face, inches away from me, listening to your occasional sigh and gurgle, I wonder how I could have ever thought glory and prizes and praise were sweeter than life.

And it's also true that I am pained, perhaps haunted is a better word, by the memory, suddenly so vivid now, of each suffering child I have come across on my journeys. To tell you the truth it's nearly too much to bear at this moment to even think of children being hurt and abused and killed. And yet looking at you the images come flooding back. Ten-year-old Andi Mikail dying from napalm burns on a hillside in Eritrea, how his voice cried out, growing ever more faint when the wind blew dust on his wounds. The two brothers, Domingo and Juste in Menongue, southern Angola. Juste, two years old and blind, dying from malnutrition, being carried on seven year old Domingo's back. And Domingo's words to me, 'He used to be nice before, but now he has the hunger'.

Last October, in Afghanistan, when you were growing inside your mother, I met Sharja, aged twelve. Motherless, fatherless, guiding me through the grey ruins of her home, everything was gone, she told me. And I knew that, for all her tender years, she had learned more about loss than I would understand in a lifetime.

There is one last memory. Of Rwanda and the churchyard of the parish of Nyarabuye where, in a ransacked classroom, I found a mother and her three young children huddled together where they'd been beaten to death. The children had died holding onto their mother, that instinct we all learn from birth and in one way or another cling to until we die.

Daniel, these memories explain some of the fierce protectiveness I feel for you, the tenderness and the occasional moments of blind terror when I imagine something happening to you. But there is something more, a story from long ago that I will tell you face to face, father to son, when you are older. It's a very personal story but it's part of the picture. It has to do with the long lines of blood and family, about our lives and how we get lost in them and, if we're lucky, find our way out again into the sunlight.

It begins thirty-five years ago in a big city on a January morning with snow on the ground and a woman walking to hospital to have her first baby. She is in her early twenties and the city is still strange to her, bigger and noisier than the easy streets and gentle hills of her distant home. She's walking because there is no money and everything of value has been pawned to pay for the alcohol to which her husband has become addicted.

On the way a taxi driver notices her sitting, exhausted and cold, in the doorway of a shop and he takes her to hospital for free. Later that day, she gives birth to a baby boy and, just as you are to me, he is the best thing she has ever seen. Her husband comes that night and weeps with joy when he sees his son. He is truly happy. Hungover, broke, but in his own way happy, for they were both young and in love with each other and their son.

But, Daniel, time had some bad surprises in store for them. The cancer of alcoholism ate away at the man and he lost his family. This was not something he meant to do or wanted to do, it just was. When you are older, my son, you will learn about how complicated life becomes, how we can lose our way and how people get hurt inside and out. By the time his son had grown up, the man lived away from his family, on his own in a one-roomed flat, living and dying for the bottle.

He died on the fifth of January, one day before the anniversary of his son's birth, all those years before in that snowbound city. But his son was too far away to hear his last words, his final breath, and all the things they might have wished to say to one another were left unspoken.

Yet now, Daniel, I must tell you that when you let out your first powerful cry in the delivery room of the Adventist Hospital and I became a father, I thought of your grandfather and, foolish though it may seem, hoped that in some way he could hear, across the infinity between the living and the dead, your proud statement of arrival. For if he could hear, he would recognise the distinct voice of family, the sound of hope and new beginnings that you and all your innocence and freshness have brought to the world.

Two letters from the heart   Class work

■   Listen to both letters being read out loud again. As you listen make brief notes on any connections you notice between the two letters. What is the effect of hearing the two letters read together? Why do you think Fergal Keane decided to publish them side by side?

■   Printed below are some words to describe the tone of a piece of autobiographical or personal writing. Look through these words and choose the ones which seem to fit both 'Letter to my Father' and 'Letter to Daniel'. Select a short quotation to illustrate each word you choose.

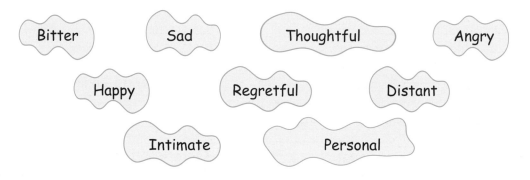

Bitter   Sad   Thoughtful   Angry

Happy   Regretful   Distant

Intimate   Personal

■   Feed back your ideas and talk about the similarities and differences. You should think about the subject and style of writing in each case.

Re-reading 'Letter to Daniel'   Homework

■   Re-read 'Letter to Daniel' and look again at your first response notes. Add any other ideas you now have.

Exploring 'Letter to Daniel'

The meaning of 'Letter to Daniel'   Class and Individual work

■   Talk about what you think the letter is about. Discuss the statements below and choose one or two that express your own view. You could make up a statement of your own.

It's a celebration of his son's birth.
It's about his relationship with his father.
It's about how his son's birth has made him think hard about his own family history.
It's about how his son's birth has made him think about other children in the world.
It's about hope for the future, both personally and in the whole world.
It's a personal piece of writing.
It's a political piece of writing.
It uses a personal story to comment on political events.

Subject	Paragraph	Comment
Hopes for his son's future		
Other children he has encountered in his work as a journalist		
His own family history		
How the birth of his son has affected him		
His immediate surroundings and career		

The structure of 'Letter to Daniel'

■ Brainstorm your first ideas about the way in which 'Letter to Daniel' is written.

■ Copy the chart above. Number each of the paragraphs in the letter.

■ Skim through the letter, looking at what Fergal Keane is writing about at different stages and fill in the second column of the chart. In the third column jot down a few words, giving a bit more detail about the paragraphs.

■ Share your discoveries about the relationship between the different sections of the letter

Getting the public's attention

■ Make a list of all the ways in which the public in this country may hear about the plight of children, in war-torn or famine-stricken countries across the world, for instance, on TV news reports. Talk about which, if any of these, makes an impact on you, what doesn't and why.

With so much news about so many different tragedies across the world, journalists and campaigners sometimes find it hard to get people to take notice of what they are reporting.

■ Make a list of the ways Fergal Keane tries to overcome this problem in *Despatches from the Heart*. Pull out the ways you find most effective. Why do you think it had such a powerful effect on people who heard it when he read it on the radio, or who bought it from bookshops? Why do you think it became a bestseller?

Finally I woke up. My body was damp with sweat. My hair was wet. I knew that I had been crying in my sleep. I turned over and grabbed the pillow to muffle out all the huge unstoppable emotion pouring out.

It must have been over an hour later when I heard the grandfather clock strike twelve noon. I calmed myself, telling my head that I must act as normal as possible so as not to arouse any suspicion. I must play my part as a normal mother. No emotion apart from the normal must be shown.

I tilted my chair. Watching my daughter playing with her cousin. The corrugated roof sheltered most of the late afternoon's sun. Their faces were happy. Was it right, I found myself suddenly wondering, to stake their lives? Suddenly I realised I was not alone. Behind me stood a woman who perhaps shared the same feeling as me – Diep, my sister-in-law. This made me feel a little better, though a twang of envy rushed through my heart. I have only one child and she has two girls and three boys who are all going. At least whatever happens, she'll be with them. As if sharing my sigh was a signal, she spoke. Sharp joy and bitterness wrapped thick in her words.

'Young, aren't they?'

'Perhaps too young.' My voice was so pained it made me jump.

'Six and seven may be the best age.'

We looked at each other, but we shared a great load. Each now lonely carries half of her burden. She walked forward. Her hand brushed over my shoulder. Her strong body walked upright. I suddenly admired her. Inside she was fire and outside she was sea. I found myself wishing with all my might that I could be like her.

The chilly wind from the sea arrived. Chills went up my spine as I decided to go in. I sat down deliberately on the cold floor. I wanted to feel solid. As solid as I could possibly get. To be on solid, not on liquid; to stay floating, not sinking. A fear of sinking has suddenly taken hold of me.

Inside the house was dead silence. Not even the dripping of taps.

The door burst open like a surprised thunderbolt followed by the laughter of children. Nai walked in, buried deep in conversation with her two cousins, Minh and Cut. Funny, I thought, the three of them nearly the same age and grown up together. And now they're going away together as well.

They seemed to be discussing a lump of sugar.

'Cut, you have it – you bought it, 'Nai volunteered.

'Why should she, she had some at home already,' Minh cried. They were interrupted by a far-off call.

'Cut, Minh, we're going to the beach now,' their mother called. Minh dragged Cut away shouting.

'Come on, we're going to the beach. Here, Nai. She shoved the sugar lump into Nai's hand. The two girls rushed out just as suddenly as they had entered.

We live quite near the sea. A trip to the seaside itself came very often but each time it did it was wholeheartedly welcomed by the children.

Nai giggled.

'Aren't they stupid, they left a whole lump of sugar behind.' She popped it into her mouth neatly. I smiled lightly. Where's she's going she'll have much more of this – much, much more. Outside I said quietly, 'Nai, I have a surprise for you. We're going to the beach too.'

The beach was deserted now. I glanced at my watch. We arrived at five o'clock. Now it was half-past seven. Just one more hour till time. The sun sank lower into the sea, dyeing it blood red. The sky was tinted with purple and orange. A few gulls cried mournfully. I leant closer to the hard body of the coconut tree. The wind blew hard, then even harder. The branches of the coconut tree bent and turned in the wind. I held on close to my daughter and hugged her even more tightly. My eyes watered. Since when it began I did not know. My face burned.

'Nai,' I said shakily, 'listen to me carefully. In a minute, daddy's boat is going to come in. You will swim out with Cut and Minh.'

'We're going to escape?' came Nai's voice excitedly.

'Yes, we're escaping. But I can't swim out. I have to go home to turn on the lights and make the people not suspicious. Then tonight daddy will come in with the boat and I'll be there.'

Why do I have to lie to her, even at this moment? I glanced at my watch. 7:45. Then my heart stopped. Voices carried by the wind reached my ears. People appeared from beyond the sand dunes. My heart leapt. Their faces were familiar and most of the voices were laughter of children. Nai immediately stood up. 'Go play with your cousins.' My sister-in-law approached me slowly. On her face I read most of her feelings. She sat down beside me, her arms folded. I glanced at my watch: exactly right.

'It's eight o'clock,' I whispered.

The figure of a man sitting across the sand must have been looking at his watch too. For at that precise moment he took out a lighter and struck. Once, twice, three times he struck at the lighter. Not once did a flame appear. He struck it again, again and again. Finally he turned toward us. The face was desperate. I felt my sister's hand grasp my arm. It tightened.

'Go, buy another one.' My voice came out hoarse and angry. The poor man jumped up and scrambled toward the street. We settled down to wait for him. I noticed even in the cold wind I was damp with perspiration.

Tension mounted in each and every one of us. We sat, each in silence, deep in our own thoughts. The children played happily on the water margin. I glanced awkwardly at my sister. I don't know why, I just felt shy. Luckily her head was buried in her hands. I felt my heart beat heavily. Every now and then I jumped nervously. Horrible thoughts crept into my mind. What if we get caught?

Slowly but steadily, time pushed on. The shadow finally came. I checked my watch again – five minutes late. The young man seemed even more nervous than I was. I had to laugh, despite the situation.

This time the lighter worked. The signal was carried out. I strained my eyes and swept my vision backwards and forwards on what I guessed was the horizon. A tiny light appeared, flashing in the darkness. This time it was I who grasped my sister-in-law. We looked at each other. Swiftly and silently, the moment had come. She stood and ran towards the water.

'Nai,' I called. She ran towards me. I think she knew the danger as well. I gathered her in my arms and held her. My heart shattered into little pieces. There was a lump in my throat.

'See you tonight,' she whispered. My throat was blocked.

'Go,' I managed to croak. Her little legs turned and accelerated. She soon reached the others. Diep, my sister-in-law, took hold of her hand. Together they entered the water. I watched their little heads bobble until they disappeared into the night. My mind and body was numb. Not a single feeling passed through.

'Goodbye,' I whispered and turned my head to remember that the sun had long gone over the horizon. I wondered silently: when will I see her again?

Giang Vo; aged 14

War reporter

Investigating a traditional news report

The report printed below is an extract from a report published in *The Daily Telegraph* in 1993, during the Bosnian War.

Listening to the report from *The Daily Telegraph*

■ Listen to the report being read aloud and jot down your first response to it. You should think about the following:
- what it is about
- who it is about
- what it focuses on
- what effect the report has on you, the reader.

Were you interested, bored, indifferent, surprised, shocked, moved emotionally?

■ Take it in turns to feed back your responses. Share anything you have noticed about the *way* the report is written.

Five die as Serbs shell busy bridge in Sarajevo
Jim Muir in Sarajevo

Bosnian Serbs killed five people and seriously injured another five when they shelled a crowded part of central Sarajevo yesterday.

The attack, the worst for three weeks, came as the head of the Muslim-dominated Bosnian presidency, Mr Alija Izetbegovic, was leaving with his delegation for talks with Bosnian Serb and Croat leaders, which open in Geneva today.

Four men died instantly, dismembered by the blast near one of the city's busiest bridges. The fifth was rushed to hospital with multiple wounds but was dead on arrival. In a separate incident, an old man was shot through the heart by a sniper and died instantly.

It was the worst day of violence in Sarajevo for nearly three weeks when seven people died including four children and their teacher.

That attack, like yesterday's was blamed on the Bosnian Serbs. UN observers record a daily catalogue of shell impacts and sniping into Sarajevo, but very little outgoing fire. Mr Izetbegovic's deputy, Ejup Ganic, accused the Bosnian Serbs of launching yesterday's attack to intensify the pressure in advance of today's talks.

But before leaving, Mr Izetbegovic said the Presidency team would continue to insist on the return of more land than was envisaged by September's plan proposed in Geneva.

He also ruled out any swapping of territory along the lines advocated by the Bosnian Serb leader, Radovan Karodzic, who wants to take over part of Sarajevo and/or the Muslim enclaves in Eastern Bosnia in exchange for other areas ...

The Daily Telegraph, **29 November, 1993**

Annotating the report   Pair and class work
- ■   Read the article again and annotate a photocopy with your ideas about the way it has been written. You should think about the following:
  -   its purpose (why it has been written; what the writer is trying to achieve)
  -   the way it is organised (the order of the ideas; the ways these are joined together)
  -   word choices, use of quotations or figures
  -   what else, if anything would you like to find out about the situation.

- ■   Agree three things to share in class discussion.

- ■   Take it in turns to offer your suggestions about the way the report is written.

Structuring a traditional report

The 'inverted pyramid'
The diagram on page 96 represents the 'inverted pyramid' structure traditionally used by newspaper journalists.

- ■   Read the diagram and take it in turns to explain to each other what it says about the way a report should be structured. For example, it suggests the most important information should be contained in the first paragraph.

- ■   Look again at Jim Muir's report and see whether or not it follows the 'inverted pyramid' structure.

- ■   Share what you have noticed with the rest of the class.

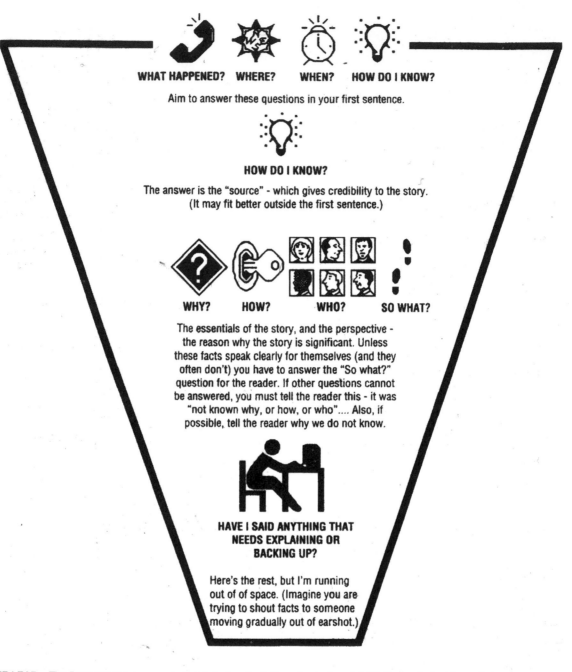

WHAT HAPPENED? **WHERE?** **WHEN?** **HOW DO I KNOW?**

Aim to answer these questions in your first sentence.

HOW DO I KNOW?

The answer is the "source" - which gives credibility to the story.
(It may fit better outside the first sentence.)

WHY? **HOW?** **WHO?** **SO WHAT?**

The essentials of the story, and the perspective -
the reason why the story is significant. Unless
these facts speak clearly for themselves (and they
often don't) you have to answer the "So what?"
question for the reader. If other questions cannot
be answered, you must tell the reader this - it was
"not known why, or how, or who".... Also, if
possible, tell the reader why we do not know.

**HAVE I SAID ANYTHING THAT
NEEDS EXPLAINING OR
BACKING UP?**

Here's the rest, but I'm running
out of of space. (Imagine you are
trying to shout facts to someone
moving gradually out of earshot.)

THE LEAD – The first sentence or paragraph. It 'tells the story'. Do not put minor detail in the lead – just the main fact.
The lead is not a summary; we need only the main point.

PYRAMID, INVERTED – as above. It tells you to put the most 'newsy' (important and/or interesting) things first; the next most newsy
things next; and so on, in descending order.

BACK-UP – Examples: If you have said that President X 'attacked' plan Y, you must then 'back this up' – in what way was it an
attack? If you have said that President X denounced the plan as a lot of nonsense, we need a full 'back-up' quote later to confirm.

Using the 'inverted structure'

■ Experiment with using the 'inverted pyramid' structure to plan a short news story.
This could be the report of something that has happened at school or at home – it
doesn't matter how trivial it is!

Writing to inform, explain and describe

New Journalism – a different kind of war reporting

Maggie O'Kane at *The Guardian* Class work

Not every journalist follows the structure of the 'inverted pyramid'. Different styles of reporting and writing can be found even in the same paper. Maggie O'Kane is one of many war reporters who writes to another set of reportage conventions, known as the 'New Journalism', which developed during the 1960s. In the quotation below, she gives her reasons for adopting this style of writing:

> I think journalism can be very boring. You are competing against a lot. There's a lot of people watching it on TV on the six o'clock news and the nine o'clock news, and then you might see it on breakfast TV. Then why on earth would you pick up *The Guardian* and read it again, unless somebody's going to tell you more about the characters, unless you're going to be told about it in a way that's entertaining, like good story-telling.

- Talk about how far you agree with the views expressed here by Maggie O'Kane. Share your expectations of her style of writing and how this might differ from a traditional report.

Comparing headlines and first paragraphs Pair work

- Jim Muir and Maggie O' Kane both filed reports on the Bosnian war on the same day in November 1993. However, the two journalists chose to report different events.

- Read the headlines and opening paragraphs of Jim Muir's report and the report written by Maggie O'Kane. What strikes you immediately about the similarities and differences in the way the two pieces begin? You should think about the following:
  - the focus of the report
  - the amount and type of information given
  - the questions it answers
  - the questions it encourages you to ask
  - your own response (for example, how you react emotionally, which you prefer and so on).

Five die as Serbs shell busy bridge in Sarajevo
Jim Muir in Sarajevo

Bosnian Serbs killed five people and seriously injured another five when they shelled a crowded part of central Sarajevo yesterday.

Desperate Bosnians risk mine-field deaths for US army rations
Maggie O'Kane in Mostar

No one knew the dead woman's name. She lay in the basement corridor of Mostar hospital for a few hours while a woman in a white bib and green overall mopped up her blood as it dripped slowly onto an icy tiled floor.

Comparing the reports

■ Write three sentences comparing the content, style and structure of the two reports. Use the connectives suggested here to help you express your ideas clearly.

Whereas	However	Nonetheless	Similarly

On the other hand	Furthermore	While

Maggie O' Kane reports

Listening to 'Desperate Bosnians'

■ Listen to the whole report being read aloud.

A personal response   Pair work

■ Talk about and prepare notes for feedback on the following:
- your first response to what she describes in her report
- whether the thoughts and feelings it prompts in you about the war, differ from those you felt on reading Jim Muir's report.

Writing to inform, explain and describe

Desperate Bosnians Risk Minefield Deaths for US Army Rations

No one knew the dead woman's name. She lay in the basement corridor of Mostar hospital for a few hours, while a woman in a white bib and green overall mopped up her blood as it dripped slowly on to an icy floor.

Her first name was Sesma. She was a refugee aged about 45. Saudin Guja met her in the crowd that flooded past his house at dawn to look for the emergency food aid dropped on the mountain by the Americans the night before.

He woke at about 5a.m as the crowd shuffled by his window searching for packages they knew had been dropped in the night from the hum of planes. He had heard nothing, but saw the crowd around Jeha Deiho's house on Ravinica hill.

He decided not to go, to stay in bed. The field was mined and only a few hundred yards from the front line with the Serbs. He was hungry but it was not worth the risk.

Blaguj has been cut off for months. The United Nations High Commissioner has not visited, and the nine-mile road that leads to Mostar can be passed only at night. Sometimes a truck makes it through from Mostar with flour and oil, but it is not enough. Saudin had not eaten for two days.

Cardboard packages left over from the gulf war, holding packets of chilli con carne and chicken a la king mix. Packages with Juicy Fruit chewing gum and brown plastic sachets of cherry and cocoa powder. Packages saying 'Made in Kansas City' in white letters.

Saudin kept telling himself the trip was too dangerous, but the returning crowd was euphoric and he was hungry. 'I saw old woman coming down the street carrying bags full of the ration packs and then I couldn't stop myself, he said.

He met Sesma just outside his front gate. He knew her as one of the refugees who had fled from the town of Stolac.

'Are the packages in Deiho's field?' she kept asking. 'It is for my children. I have nothing to cook for them. No food.'

They walked quickly. She talked about her children. He wondered if there would be anything left. On the way up, they were passed by two soldiers carrying an old man. His leg had been blown off in a mine in Deiho's field.

As they reached the field, they saw another explosion in the distance. A mine detonated by someone else scavenging for packages.

They kept going. Sesma kept talking about her children being hungry. He nodded, let her ramble on. As they reached the field, the Bosnian soldiers called out to them: 'Don't go on, the field is mined.'

But nobody listened. They were calling to us: 'The Chetniks [Serbian soldiers] are at the end of the field, stay away.'

But the people ran deeper and deeper into the minefield.

Another woman, a 22 year-old local called Colla, passed them on a stretcher. She had reached the hill at 5a.m and picked her way carefully thought he field. But looking up, she saw a woman about to step on a mine and called out to her to watch out. Then one exploded under her feet, breaking the bones.

Sesma and Saudin had gathered about twelve packages when he heard shouts from the end of the field. 'Come on you Muslims. Come on over here and we'll give you some food.'

'The Chetniks were laughing at us,' Saudin said. Five Serb soldiers walked towards them. 'Come on Muslims, Get your American parcels.'

They panicked. Sesma was running about five feet in front of him when she hit the mine. It blew her apart.

A second later, he felt the blast under his foot. He heard Sesma beside him. When she was dying, she kept repeating: 'My children, my children.'

They buried her at night in Mostar graveyard, wrapped in a brown wool blanket, in a coffin made from teak veneer wardrobe. On it, they wrote: 'Sesma'. No one knew anything else about the refugee from the Stolac who died on the mountain.

Maggie O'Kane, *The Guardian*
29th Nov 1993

Printed below are some statements about Maggie O'Kane's report.

■ Use them as a starting point for discussing the report. Make sure you look back at the report to find evidence for what you are saying.

Maggie O'Kane represents the 'voice' of the ordinary people.

Although Maggie O'Kane wasn't in the minefield, the report is very immediate.

The report is powerful because it is understated.

The report uses plain language with very few adverbs or adjectives.

There is very little commentary from Maggie O'Kane,

Sharing your ideas Class work

■ Take it in turns to share your comments on the report.

Writing about Maggie O'Kane's report Homework

■ Use the statements and the ideas you talked about in the class discussion to help you write your own paragraph about Maggie O'Kane's report.

Writing to inform, explain and describe

Conventions of New Journalism

Telling it like a story   Class work

Maggie O'Kane suggests that one problem a newspaper journalist has is actually getting someone to read a newspaper - especially when there is TV, radio, the internet and so on, all providing instant access to the news.

- Talk about whether you think she does make the reader sit up and take notice of what she has written. Identify two places where you think she has been successful and choose a short quotation which demonstrates this.

As Maggie O'Kane explains, her style of journalism is to 'tell it like a story'.

Maggie O'Kane on Journalism   Class viewing

- Listen to Maggie O'Kane's explanation of how she writes the news like story. Note down as many of the techniques she mentions as you can. You may have to watch it more than once.

Exploring the report   Pair and class work

- Skim read the report again and find one quotation to show each technique she mentions. In your own words, explain how the technique works and why it is an effective way of telling readers about the war.

Re-writing a traditional report

- Read Jim Muir's report again and talk about some of the ways you could re-write the first two paragraphs in the style of Maggie O'Kane's report.

Writing in the style of Muir and O'Kane   Homework

- Write the opening paragraph of a newspaper report on a current news issue in the style of each writer (Jim Muir and Maggie O'Kane).

The Bosnian war as a graphic novel

Joe Sacco is an American artist who has written a graphic novel called *Safe Area Gorazde* which depicts life in the Bosnian town of Gorazde in the early 90s. 'Safe havens' were parts of the country that the UN were supposed to be protecting from the Serbian army. The UN often failed to do this. Srebrenica and Zepa are just two of the more famous examples. Joe Sacco's book tells of another, barely reported example of this failure to protect innocent civilians.

How do you respond?   Class and pair work

■   Look at the extract on page 103 and talk about your first reaction to the story it tells. What do you find most striking about this text?

■   How does your reaction to this extract compare with your reaction to the two news reports you have read?

How does this text work?

Here is a list of some of the techniques used in this graphic novel that one reader noticed. Talk about the way they are used and the effect they have on the reader. Add any other techniques you notice and which you think are particularly effective.

- Personal voice
- Narrator telling the story
- Font like a child's handwriting
- Use of perspective to draw the eye across the page
- Photographic technique – a long shot to show the extent of the slaughter
- Use of camera angles and viewpoints like a film – moving from high to low angles
- A range of different eyewitness voices like a documentary
- Emphasis on the pain of the victim personalises the horror

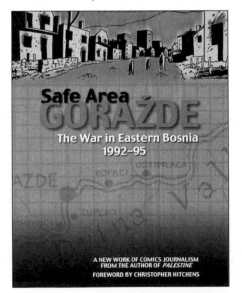

Safe Area **GORAŹDE**
The War in Eastern Bosnia
1992–95

A NEW WORK OF COMICS JOURNALISM
FROM THE AUTHOR OF *PALESTINE*
FOREWORD BY CHRISTOPHER HITCHENS

From *Safe Area Gorazde* by Joe Sacco

Same war, different stories

■ Compare the war stories from *The Daily Telegraph*, *The Guardian* and the graphic novel, *Safe Area Gorazde*.

■ List the strengths and weaknesses of each in terms of the way they present of the Bosnian war and your reaction to each text. Use a grid like the one below to record your ideas.

	Jim Muir: *The Daily Telegraph*	Maggie O'Kane: *The Guardian*	Joe Sacco: *Safe Area Gorazde*
Strengths			
Weaknesses			
Your reaction			
3 techniques used			
Purpose			
Audience			

A personal response to stories of war   Homework

■ Write a short, personal piece summarising your response to the three texts on the Bosnian War.

Reporting the news in the style of Maggie O' Kane

Writing to a deadline   Individual work

Journalists working to very tight deadlines deliver their 'copy' by phone or email. If they don't make the deadline, the paper goes to press without their piece and editors won't want to use their work again. As Maggie O'Kane makes clear, although journalists research and plan their pieces very carefully and in detail, they often don't have time to do lots of drafts. This is your chance to have a go at writing without drafting. You will write a report of about 200-500 words in the style of Maggie O'Kane.

Telling a story   Pair and individual work

■ Take it in turns to tell each other about a time when you were very frightened. Perhaps you were in a fight or you saw something that shocked or scared you. Your account should be as full and as detailed as possible.

■ As you listen to your partner's story, make sure you note down the main points.

Writing to inform, explain and describe

Planning and drafting your report

■　Think through the following stages to make sure you meet the deadline and sell your story.

- Find an angle
- Choose a focus (for example, a character)
- Plan the structure
- Write the first and last paragraphs.

■　Plan your piece, paragraph by paragraph. Write notes to remind yourself of any facts, details or quotations you want to include. You could also make a list of words which you think will help your readers picture the scene or understand the issue.

■　Write your story.

Editing

Once written, the report goes to an editor. Editors make sure the report makes sense and is the right number of words. They also add the headline. This needs both to attract the attention of the reader and to give some idea of what the report is about.

■　Work together to edit each other's reports.

Listening to the reports   Class work

■　Listen to a few of the reports and talk about what you have learned about the different ways in which you can tell a news story.

A final report   Homework

■　Write up your news report as a piece of writing to inform, describe and explain.

Dilemmas

In this unit you will:
- explore the issues around a difficult topic
- develop and defend a point of view
- take account of the views of others
- read editorials and articles that attempt to persuade the reader of a particular point of view
- practise writing your own argument or persuasion piece.

Confronting a Dilemma

What is a dilemma?   Class and group work
- Talk about what you understand by the word 'dilemma'. Share your own experiences of being in a dilemma.

What would you do?
- Deciding what is right and what is wrong can be very difficult. It is not always clear what is the right decision.

- Read the dilemma printed below.

- Talk about your opinions of the situation. What do you think you would do if confronted with this dilemma or asked to make a judgement about it? Do you think the survivor was right or wrong?

Two shipwrecked people were struggling in the water. One was holding on to a plank and the other swimming towards it. The plank would not keep two people afloat, so the one who had reached the plank first pushed back the other, who subsequently drowned.
The survivor was accused of murder and tried in court.

Defending a viewpoint
If you were on the jury or if you were the judge what decision would you take about the survivor's guilt or innocence?

- Divide the classroom into three areas:
'Agree', 'Disagree', 'Don't Know'. Go to the area of the room that best sums up your views about the statement:
The survivor was guilty of murder.

Writing to persuade and argue

■ Take it in turns for the people in the 'Agree' and 'Disagree' areas to try to persuade the people in the 'Don't Know' area to come over to their point of view. The people in the 'Don't Know' section should challenge any aspects of the argument they are not convinced by or which they feel to be unreliable. If anyone changes their mind, they should move to a different area of the room.

What really happened?

The dilemma you have just discussed is a true story. In the court case the survivor was acquitted (found not guilty). The reason was that 'the law recognises that a person who is in the position of having a reasonable chance to survive cannot be expected to give up his life to save another or to share the fate of death'.

■ Spend a few minutes talking about this judgement and the difficult issues it raises.

Revising the language of persuasion and argument

■ Brainstorm some of the words and phrases you used to put forward your point of view. Use the examples suggested here to get you started.

Don't you realise?

That's just stupid!

No, no, listen!

It's obvious

■ Talk about which kinds of persuasive language you found most effective. Which kinds of persuasive language did you find least effective?

Practising written argument   Individual work

In writing, the language of argument and persuasion is often more formal, tentative and reasonable than spoken arguments. This is true even when the writer is putting forward just one point of view rather than a balanced argument. A writer may use words and phrases like the ones suggested here:

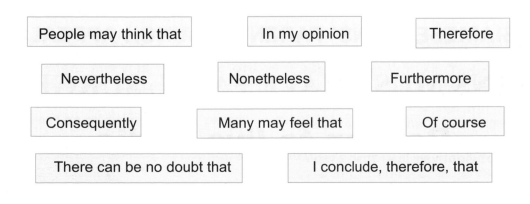

People may think that   In my opinion   Therefore

Nevertheless   Nonetheless   Furthermore

Consequently   Many may feel that   Of course

There can be no doubt that   I conclude, therefore, that

7 Everyone has the right to life, whether they are disabled or not. Surgery would mean the death of the daughter, Mary.

8 Once a child is born, a parent's right to choose (open to them before birth in the form of contraception and abortion) is no longer open to them. If babies are denied life because they are deemed unsuitable or imperfect, then we are only a step away from the dying rooms of China, where sick children in orphanages are simply allowed to waste away.

9 It is against God's will to allow the operation. It is God's will that the twins be born with the afflictions they have and they should be left to live their lives joined together, however long that shall be.

10 Parents should have the right to decide what happens to their children. The parents wishes should be respected.

11 Jodie is entitled to protest that Mary is killing her. Nobody but the doctors can help Jodie. Mary sadly is beyond any help. The best interests of the twins is to give the chance of life to the child whose actual bodily condition is capable of accepting the chance to her advantage even if that has to be at the cost of the sacrifice of a life which is so unnaturally supported.

12 There are serious questions about the quality of Jodie's life after the operation. The operation will not be without risk to Jodie's life as well.

13 The legal reality here, harsh as it is to state it and unnatural as it is that it should be happening, is that Mary is killing Jodie.

14 If you can save one life by acting, but lose two by doing nothing, then of course you should act.

15 It could be argued that Jodie and Mary are really 'one life' not two because without Jodie, Mary would not be alive.

16 If the operation goes ahead and the weaker twin dies (as seems inevitable), her death will not have been caused by the surgeons. It will have been caused by the impossible condition with which she was born. That is a result of biology, not of human intervention.

A newspaper report - is it the whole story?

The writer's position on the dilemma Class work

■ Listen to the article from the *Daily Mirror* and talk about the position the writer takes towards the dilemma.

■ Look at the words listed here. Talk about the ones which you think could be used to describe the article from the *Daily Mirror*.

informative   reliable   opinionated   biased

subjective   balanced   authoritative

convincing   reasonable   informed

Jill Palmer on why it's right to keep fighting for Jodie

It was an agonising decision but to my mind it was the right one. The judges' ruling means that one baby will be given the chance of survival.

Yet it is no time for celebration. For the other child is sadly condemned to certain death.

And although the doctors who fought for the right to operate will be relieved and pleased their delight will be tinged with distress at being forced to go against the parents' wishes.

The real winner is Jodie. She is being given the chance which, without the operation, she could never have.

Of course, she may not survive the complex surgery. But that is no excuse not to try. It would be scandalous if doctors did not attempt to save lives or operate on patients just because they thought they may not be successful. Tragically Jodie is likely to be disabled. She may need treatment for the rest of her life. But there would be a public outcry if doctors abandoned babies just because they were disabled.

Surgeons agree that to give Jodie the best

chance the operation should go ahead by the second week of October.

If the parents continue to fight they could still lose and at the same time rob Jodie of her best chances.

The ordeal of the birth and this court action is something the parents will never forget. They should now try and put it behind them and concentrate on Jodie's survival. Of course they will mourn the daughter they lost.

But everything possible must be done to help the daughter they have gained.

The Daily Mirror **23.9.00**

Fact and opinion   Pair and group work

■   Read the article again and on a chart like the one below record the 'Facts' and 'Opinions' used in the article.

■   Join up with another pair and compare your record of facts and opinions. Talk about how this writer combines fact and opinion.

Facts	Opinions	Unsure

Challenging the article

It is very easy to be convinced by an article like this one and to accept that, because it is published in a newspaper, it offers all the facts. Is this true?

■   Read the article again and make a note of the following:
-   the assumptions it makes
-   doubts you have about the facts or the way they are presented
-   the conclusion which the writer draws from the facts
-   further information which you need to come to an informed opinion
-   any other points you would like to challenge the writer about.

■   Feed back what you have discovered about the balance between the facts and opinions in the article. Share your thoughts on the ways in which the arguments could be challenged or questioned.

Evaluating the article   Homework

■   Summarise your evaluation of the article by explaining how effective you think it is as a text which:
-   informs
-   persuades
-   argues
-   entertains.

■   Does what you have discovered about the article make you read it in a different way?

Extension Work - exploring editorial writing

Newspaper editorials do not claim to provide a balanced view of a subject. The editorial writer argues one side of a case.

The key points   Class work

Printed below are three key sentences from *The Guardian* editorial.

> No, given the age and vulnerability of both the twins, this case has to be regarded as a question of private morality, leaving the state no right to intervene.

> The case of the Siamese twins, Jodie and Mary, is a parent's worst nightmare.

> But the crux of this case is not to be found in such legal issues, but in a broader consideration of what is in the best interests of all - both parents and children.

- Put the sentences into the order you think they appear in the editorial. Talk about how you decided which one is taken from the introduction, which from the conclusion and which from the middle of the piece.

- What do you think this piece is arguing?

Reading the editorial

- Listen to the editorial below being read aloud, making brief notes on anything which strikes you as important or interesting.

- Take a few minutes to skim read the piece again and talk about the position the writer takes on the argument.

The cruellest choice

A decision for parents, not for the state

The case of the Siamese twins, Jodie and Mary, is a parent's worst nightmare. Jodie, according to evidence in the court hearings, is a 'bright and alert baby, sparkling and sucking on her dummy'; her sister Mary's state is 'pitiable' - she cannot even cry, because she has no lungs of her own. Mary depends on Jodie for her blood and oxygen. She is incapable of independent life but is slowly draining her conjoined sister, and unless they are separated, both will die within six months. The doctors in charge of the case want to save Jodie, which would mean killing Mary. The parents insist that God's will be done and that nature should be left to take its course. The only way to resolve the deadlock in this agonising dilemma has been to resort to the courts. Not surprisingly, the appeal court judges and the barristers admit to sleepless nights as they wrestle with the ethical and emotional implications.

Part of that perhaps arises from the sense that the law is not the right arbiter in this extremely unusual and delicate situation. The parents and the official solicitor acting on Mary's behalf have appealed against the high court decision for the operation to go ahead and the lawyers are debating fine legal points along the murky boundary between what is an unlawful killing and what constitutes 'withdrawal of treatment'.   But the crux of this case is not to be found in such legal issues, but in a broader consideration of what is in the best interests of all - both parents and children.

It seems common sense that the right thing to do is to save one life, rather than lose both. But it is also common sense that the parents' wishes lie at the heart of the case. The Manchester hospital where the children are being treated has been inundated by members of the public protesting at the parents being overruled in the high-court judgement. Of course, in some cases we understand that parents' rights can be superseded by the state's responsibility to protect children's rights; for example, the state can overrule a Jehovah's Witness parent's refusal to allow a healthy child to have a blood transfusion.

But this is not such a case. In addition to the anguish the parents feel at one of their daughters dying and their own moral objections to this as devout Catholics, the benefits for Jodie are not even clear. There are serious questions about the quality of Jodie's life after the operation; the parents are certain that the health service in their home country and their financial situation would prevent them from caring properly for her if she was seriously disabled. They would perhaps have to leave her behind for fostering in England. In such circumstances how can the court enforce the operation even if it is ethically the right thing to do? After all, it will be the parents who will be left to carry the can. No, given the age and vulnerability of both the twins, this case has to be regarded as a question of private morality, leaving the state no right to intervene.

The Guardian

The features of an editorial
Listed below are some of the key features of an editorial.
- How many of them did you notice in this example?

    Editorials are often short – no more than 3 or 4 paragraphs.
    They deliberately present one point of view.
    Their purpose is to persuade the reader to that point of view.
    They have a clear idea of their target audience – and what their opinions are likely to be on a wide range of subjects.
    Paragraphs often only have one or two sentences.
    The conclusion either raises a provocative question or is a call for action.

Exploring the structure of the editorial   Pair work
- Look closely at the ways the writer leads the reader through the arguments. Find at least one example of each technique listed here and, in your own words, explain how each one helps the reader understand the argument.

A personal view
A sense of conviction
Use of rhetorical questions
Use of repetition
Use of tentative, reasoned persuasion such as: perhaps, it seems, of course
Use of modal verbs suggesting possibility rather than certainty for example: would, should
Use of terms which signpost the development of the line of thought for example:
but, not surprisingly, after all, of course, the only way
Use of quotation
Use of facts
Development of an argument in a series of logical steps
Anticipation of responses and objections

Listening to the analyses Class work

- Listen to one or two of the analyses in detail and take it in turns to suggest any other points which have not been mentioned already.

Two sides of the argument Homework

- Skim read both the article from *The Mirror* and *The Guardian* editorial again.

- Which piece of writing do you find the most persuasive and why? For example, is it because you already agree with the position taken? Or is it because the writer has drawn together facts you cannot argue against? Or because the writer has put forward the argument and his or her opinion in a persuasive manner?

Presenting a point of view – a lawyer's speech

Revising the language of argument Class work
You have already looked at some ways of expressing a point of view in spoken and written arguments.

- Remind yourselves of the key words and phrases in argument writing. Talk about the way arguments might be expressed differently in a court of law. Use the phrases suggested here to get you started:
  I put it to you that …
  It has been stated that …

Preparing the lawyer role play Group work
Your teacher will give different groups the task of preparing the arguments either for or against the separation. One person from each group will be asked to deliver the speech to the rest of the class, in the role of a lawyer.

- Re-read all the facts, opinions and arguments selecting those which support your case or which reveal the opposition's argument as flawed or mistaken.

■   Make a note of any words or phrases which might help you express your arguments in a logical and convincing way. Use the questions listed here to help you organise your argument.

-    What do you want to persuade your listeners to think?
-    What are the three key points of your argument? Can you map them out as a flow chart?
-    What would be a good opening sentence?
-    What would be a good final sentence?
-    Which words will you use to signpost the argument?
-    How will you join your ideas together?
-    How will you use the facts of the case?
-    How will you use the different expert opinions (for example, will you quote them in your speech, refer to them in detail, call them as a witness)?
-    What sort of language will you use (for example, calm, emotional)?
-    How will you deliver your speech? (Think about tone of voice, relationship with your listener, gestures, body language and so on.)

You could begin your speech like this:
'Your honour, this is indeed a tragic and unique case … '

Delivering the argument
■   Listen to the arguments put by the different groups of lawyers. As you listen make a note of the arguments you find persuasive and any points where you think the speaker is misusing the evidence or making a claim that can't be backed up.
Sharing your responses
■   Share your responses to the lawyers' presentations.

The judge's summing up – presenting a balanced case   Homework
■   Use what you have learned about the dilemma of the conjoined twins to write the judge's final summing up of the case. You should include:

-    an overview of the dilemma
-    a summary of the arguments for and against the separation
-    quotations from experts
-    a final recommendation.

The words and phrases suggested here will help you balance one argument against another.

It has been suggested …
However, we must also take into account…
It has been pointed out …
We have been made aware of …
This has been a difficult case. The conclusion I have come to is that …

Stephen King

Exploring fiction and non-fiction

How well do you know Stephen King's writing?   Group work

Stephen King is one of the most popular writers alive today. Many of his novels have been adapted for the screen.

■ Look at the collection of book covers below and discuss what you have read or seen of his work. You could organise your ideas about Stephen King under the headings suggested here.

Three things I know about Stephen King's work:
Three things I like (or do not like) about Stephen King's work:

Fiction or non-fiction?   Pair work

Stephen King is famous for writing fiction, particularly horror fiction. However, the focus of this unit of work is a piece of non-fiction that he wrote in 2000 called 'The Accident'. In each of the three pairs of extracts printed below, one is taken from his non-fiction writing, 'The Accident' and one is a taken from the beginning of his novel, *Misery*.

■   Share your ideas about the differences between fiction and non-fiction texts.

■   Read one of the pairs of extracts and decide which one is fiction and which one is non-fiction. Talk about how you made your decision. If you found it difficult to decide, talk about why this was.

A1. *Help is on the way*, I think, and that's probably good because I've been in a hell of an accident. I'm lying in the ditch and there's blood all over my face and my right leg hurts. I look down and see something I don't like: my lap now appears to be on sideways, as if my whole lower body had been wrenched half a turn to the right.

A2. But sometimes the sounds – like the pain – faded, and then there was only the haze. He remembered the darkness: solid darkness had come before the haze. Did that mean he was making progress?

B2.   When she took her lips away this time he did not let her breath out but *pushed* it and whooped in a gigantic breath of his own. Shoved it out. Waited for his unseen chest to go up again on its own, as it had been doing his whole life without any help from him. When it didn't, he gave another giant whooping gasp, and then he was breathing again on his own, and doing it as fast as he could to flush the smell and taste of her out of him.

Normal air had never tasted so fine.

B1.   'Feel like I'm drowning.' I whisper.

Somebody checks something, and someone else says, 'His lung has collapsed.'

There's a rattle of paper as something is unwrapped, and then the someone else speaks into my ear, loudly so as to be heard over the rotors. 'We're going to put a chest tube in you. You'll feel some pain, a little pinch. Hold on.'

It's like being thumped very high up on the right side of the chest by someone holding a short sharp object. Then there's an alarming whistle in my chest, as if I've sprung a leak. In fact, I suppose I have. A moment later, the soft in-out of normal respiration, which I've listened to my whole life (mostly without being aware of it, thank God), has been replaced by an unpleasant *schoop-schloop-schloop* sound. The air I'm taking is very cold, but it's air, at least, air, and I keep breathing it. I don't want to die.

C1. I ask him if I'm going to die. He tells me no, I'm not going to die, but I need to go to the hospital, and fast. I ask Fillebrown again if I'm going to die, and he tells me again that I'm not. Then he asks me if I can wriggle the toes on my right foot. 'My toes, did they move?' I ask Paul Fillebrown. He says they did, a good healthy wriggle. 'Do you swear to God?' I ask him, and I think he does. I'm starting to pass out again. Fillebrown asks me, very slowly and loudly, bending down into my face, if my wife is at the big house on the lake. I can't remember.

C2. For some length of time that seemed very long (and so *was*, since the pain and the stormy haze were the only two things which existed) those sounds were the only outer reality. He had no idea who he was or where he was and cared to know neither. He wished he was dead, but through the pain-soaked haze that filled his mind like a summer storm-cloud, he did not know he wished it.

Sharing your ideas　Class work
- Read the extracts out loud and take it in turns to report back briefly on your discussion.

Your teacher will tell you which extracts are from the novel *Misery* and which are from the non-fiction recount, 'The Accident'.

- Share your responses to what you are told. Do these pieces by Stephen King confirm or challenge your ideas about fiction and non-fiction?

Reading 'The Accident'
- Listen to 'The Accident' being read aloud. Your teacher will stop reading three or four times so that you can comment on what you noticed about the writing. Your teacher will give you responsibility for concentrating on one of the following as you listen:
- the way that characters are described
- the way that places are described
- the way that thoughts and feelings are described
- the way that physical and medical details are explained.
- the way that Stephen King keeps the reader interested (for example by increasing tension)
- the structure of 'The Accident'. (Is it a chronological recount or does it move backwards and forwards in time?)

- Take it in turns to feed back to the whole class examples of what you noticed while you were listening.

- Talk about any features of fiction writing that Stephen King uses in 'The Accident'.

'There are confused
glimpses of faces
and operating
rooms; there
are delusions
and hallucinations.
Mostly, though,
there is darkness'

In our second extract from Stephen King's new book,
On Writing, the best-selling author recalls the day a
country walk turned into a horrifying fight for survival

The accident

When we're at our summer house in western
Maine, I walk four miles every day, unless it's
pouring down with rain. Three miles of this walk
are on dirt roads which wind through the
woods; a mile of it is on Route 5, a two-lane
blacktop highway which runs between Bethel
and Fryeburg.

The third week in June of 1999 was an
extraordinarily happy one for my wife and me;
our kids, now grown and scattered across the
country, were all home. It was the first time in
nearly six months that we'd all been under the
same roof. As an extra bonus, our first
grandchild was in the house, three months old
and happily jerking at a helium balloon tied to
his foot.

On 19 June, I drove our younger son to the
Portland Jetport, where he caught a flight back
to New York City. I drove home, had a brief
nap, and then set out on my usual walk. We
were planning to go en famille to see *The
General's Daughter* in nearby North Conway,
New Hampshire that evening, and I thought I
just had time to get my walk in before packing
everybody up for the trip.

I set out on that walk around four o'clock in
the afternoon, as well as I can remember. Just
before reaching the main road (in western
Maine, any road with a white line running down
the middle of it is a main road), I stepped into
the woods and urinated. It was two months
before I was able to take another leak standing up.

When I reached the highway I turned north,
walking on the gravel shoulder, against traffic.
One car passed me, also headed north. About
three-quarters of a mile farther along, the
woman driving the car observed a light-blue
Dodge van heading south. The van was
looping from one side of the road to the other,
barely under the driver's control. The woman
in the car turned to her passenger when they
were safely past the wandering van and said,
'That was Stephen King walking back there. I
sure hope that guy in the van doesn't hit him.'

Most of the sightlines along the mile of Route
5 which I walk are good, but there is one
stretch, a short, steep hill, where a pedestrian
walking north can see very little of what might
be coming his way. I was three-quarters of the
way up this hill when Bryan Smith, the owner

and operator of the light-blue Dodge van, came over the crest.

He wasn't on the road; he was on the shoulder. My shoulder. I had perhaps three-quarters of a second to register this. It was just time enough to think, My God, I'm going to be hit by a school bus. I started to turn to my left. There is a break in my memory here. On the other side of it, I'm on the ground, looking at the back of the van, which is now pulled off the road and tilted to one side.

This recollection is very clear and sharp, more like a snapshot than a memory. There is dust around the van's tail-lights. The licence plate and the back windows are dirty. I register these things with no thought that I have been in an accident, or of anything else. It's a snapshot, that's all. I'm not thinking; my head has been swopped clean.

There's another little break in my memory here, and then I am very carefully wiping palmfuls of blood out of my eyes with my left hand. When my eyes are reasonably clear, I look around and see a man sitting on a nearby rock. He has a cane drawn across his lap. This is Bryan Smith, 42 years of age, the man who hit me with his van. Smith has got quite a driving record; he has racked up nearly a dozen vehicle-related offences.

Smith wasn't looking at the road on the afternoon our lives came together, because his Rottweiler had jumped from the very rear of his van into the back-seat area, where there was an Igloo cooler with some meat stored inside. The Rottweiler's name is Bullet (Smith has another Rottweiler at home; that one is named Pistol). Bullet started to nose at the lid of the cooler. Smith turned around and tried to push Bullet away. He was still looking at Bullet and pushing his head away from the cooler when he came over the top of the knoll; still looking and pushing when he struck me.

Smith told friends later that he thought he'd hit 'a small deer' until he noticed my bloody

spectacles lying on the front seat of his van. They were knocked from my face when I tried to get out of Smith's way. The frames were bent and twisted, but the lenses were unbroken. They are the lenses I'm wearing now, as I write this.

Smith sees I'm awake and tells me help is on the way. He speaks calmly, even cheerily. His look, as he sits on his rock with his cane drawn across his lap, is one of pleasant commiseration: Ain't the two of us just had the shittiest luck? it says. He and Bullet left the campground where they were staying, he later tells an investigator, because he wanted 'some of those Marzes-bars they have up to the store'. When I hear this little detail some weeks later, it occurs to me that I have nearly been killed by a character right out of one of my own novels. It's almost funny.

Help is on the way, I think, and that's probably good because I've been in a hell of an accident. I'm lying in the ditch and there's blood all over my face and my right leg hurts. I look down and see something I don't like: my lap now appears to be on sideways, as if my whole lower body had been wrenched half a turn to the right. I look back up at the man with the cane and say, 'Please tell me it's just dislocated.'

'Nah,' he says. Like his face, his voice is cheery, only mildly interested. He could be watching all this on TV while he noshes on one of those Marzes-bars. 'It's broken in five I'd say maybe six places.' 'I'm sorry,' I tell him - God knows why - and then I'm gone again for a little while. It isn't like blacking out; it's more as if the film of memory has been spliced here and there.

When I come back this time, an orange-and-white van is idling at the side of the road with its flashers going. An emergency medical technician - Paul Fillebrown is his name - is kneeling beside me. He's doing something. Cutting off my jeans, I think, although that might have come later.

I ask him if I can have a cigarette. He laughs and says not hardly. I ask him if I'm going to die. He tells me no, I'm not going to die, but I need to go to the hospital, and fast. I ask Fillebrown again if I'm going to die, and he tells me again that I'm not. Then he asks me if I can wiggle the toes on my right foot. 'My toes, did they move?' I ask Paul Fillebrown. He says they did, a good healthy wiggle. 'Do you swear to God?' I ask him, and I think he does. I'm starting to pass out again. Fillebrown asks me, very slowly and loudly, bending down into my face, if my wife is at the big house on the lake. I can't remember. I can't remember where any of my family is, but I'm able to give him the telephone numbers of both our big house and the cottage on the far side of the lake where my daughter sometimes stays. Hell, I could give him my Social Security number, if he asked. I've got all my numbers. It's just everything else that's gone.

Other people are arriving now. Somewhere a radio is crackling out police calls. I'm put on a stretcher. It hurts, and I scream. I'm lifted into the back of the EMT truck, and the police calls are closer. The doors shut and someone up front says, 'You want to really hammer it.' Then we're rolling.

Paul Fillebrown sits down beside me. He has a pair of clippers and tells me he's going to have to cut the ring off the third finger of my right hand - it's a wedding ring Tabby gave me in 1983, 12 years after we were actually married. I try to tell Fillebrown that I wear it on my right hand because the real wedding ring is still on the third finger of my left - the original two-ring set cost me $15.95 at Day's Jewelers in Bangor. That first ring only cost eight bucks, in other words, but it seems to have worked. Some garbled version of this comes out, probably nothing Paul Fillebrown can actually understand, but he keeps nodding and smiling as he cuts that second, more expensive, wedding ring off my swollen right hand. Two months or so later, I call Fillebrown to thank him; by then I understand that he probably saved my life by administering the correct on-scene medical aid and then getting me to the hospital at a speed of roughly 110mph, over patched and bumpy back roads.

Fillebrown assures me that I'm more than welcome, then suggests that perhaps someone was watching out for me. 'I've been doing this for 20 years,' he tells me over the phone, 'and when I saw the way you were lying in the ditch, plus the extent of the impact injuries, I didn't think you'd make it to the hospital. You're a lucky camper to still be with the program.'

The extent of the impact injuries is such that the doctors at Northern Cumberland Hospital decide they cannot treat me there; someone summons a LifeFlight helicopter to take me to Central Maine Medical Center in Lewiston. At this point my wife, older son, and daughter arrive. The kids are allowed a brief visit; my wife is allowed to stay longer. The doctors have assured her that I'm banged up, but I'll make it. The lower half of my body has been covered. She isn't allowed to look at the interesting way my lap has shifted around to the right, but she is allowed to wash the blood off my face and pick some of the glass out of my hair. There's a long gash in my scalp, the result of my collision with Bryan Smith's windshield. This impact came at a point less than two inches from the steel, driver's-side support post. Had I struck that, I likely would have been killed or rendered permanently comatose, a vegetable with legs. Had I struck the rocks jutting out of the ground beyond the shoulder of Route 5, I likely also would have been killed or permanently paralysed. I didn't hit them; I was thrown over the van and 14ft in the air, but landed just shy of the rocks.

'You must have pivoted to the left just a little at the last second,' Dr David Brown tells me later. 'If you hadn't, we wouldn't be having this conversation.'

The Life Flight helicopter lands in the parking lot of Northern Cumberland Hospital, and I am wheeled out to it. The sky is very bright, very blue. The clatter of the helicopter's rotors is very loud. Someone shouts into my ear, 'Ever been in a helicopter before, Stephen?' The speaker sounds jolly, all excited for me. I try to answer yes, I've been in a helicopter before - twice, in fact - but I can't. All at once, it's very tough to breathe.

They load me into the helicopter. I can see one brilliant wedge of blue sky as we lift off; not a cloud in it. Beautiful. There are more radio voices. This is my afternoon for hearing voices, it seems. Meanwhile, it's getting even harder to breathe. I gesture at someone, or try to, and a face bends upside down into my field of vision.

'Feel like I'm drowning,' I whisper.

Somebody checks something, and someone else says, 'His lung has collapsed.'

There's a rattle of paper as something is unwrapped, and then the someone else speaks into my ear, loudly so as to be heard over the rotors. 'We're going to put a chest tube in you, Stephen. You'll feel some pain, a little pinch. Hold on.'

It's like being thumped very high up on the right side of the chest by someone holding a short sharp object. Then there's an alarming whistle in my chest, as if I've sprung a leak. In fact, I suppose I have. A moment later, the soft in-out of normal respiration, which I've listened to my whole life (mostly without being aware of it, thank God), has been replaced by an unpleasant shloop-shloop-shloop sound. The air I'm taking in is very cold, but it's air, at least, air, and I keep breathing it. I don't want to die. I love my wife, my kids, my afternoon walks by the lake. I also love to write. I don't want to die, and as I lie in the helicopter looking out at the bright blue summer sky, I realise that I am actually lying in death's doorway. Someone is going to pull me one way or the other pretty

soon; it's mostly out of my hands. All I can do is lie there, look at the sky, and listen to my thin, leaky breathing: shloop-shloop-shloop.

Ten minutes later, we set down on the concrete landing pad at CMMC. To me, it seems to be at the bottom of a concrete well. The blue sky is blotted out and the whap-whap-whap of the helicopter rotors becomes magnified and echoey, like the clapping of giant hands.

Still breathing in great leaky gulps, I am lifted out of the helicopter. Someone bumps the stretcher and I scream. 'Sorry, sorry, you're okay, Stephen,' someone says - when you're badly hurt, everyone calls you by your first name, everyone is your pal.

'Tell Tabby I love her very much,' I say as I am first lifted and then wheeled, very fast, down some sort of descending concrete walkway. All at once I feel like crying.

'You can tell her that yourself,' the someone says. We go through a door; there is air-conditioning and lights flowing past overhead. Speakers issue pages. It occurs to me, in a muddled sort of way, that an hour before I was taking a walk and planning to pick some berries in a field that overlooks Lake Kezar. I wouldn't pick for long, though; I'd have to be home by 5.30 because we were all going to the movies. *The General's Daughter* , starring John Travolta. Travolta was in the movie made out of *Carrie*, my first novel. He played the bad guy. That was a long time ago.

'When?' I ask. 'When can I tell her?'

'Soon,' the voice says, and then I pass out again. This time it's no splice but a great big whack taken out of the memory-film; there are a few flashes, confused glimpses of faces and operating rooms and looming X-ray machinery; there are delusions and hallucinations fed by the morphine and Dilaudid being dripped into me; there are echoing voices and hands that reach down to paint my dry lips with swabs that taste of peppermint. Mostly, though, there is darkness.

Bryan Smith's estimate of my injuries turned out to be conservative. My lower leg was broken in at least nine places - the orthopaedic surgeon who put me together again, the formidable David Brown, said that the region below my right knee had been reduced to 'so many marbles in a sock.'

The extent of those lower-leg injuries necessitated two deep incisions - they're called medial and lateral fasciatomies - to release the pressure caused by the exploded tibia and also to allow blood to flow back into the lower leg. Without the fasciatomies (or if the fasciatomies had been delayed), it probably would have been necessary to amputate the leg. My right knee itself was split almost directly down the middle; the technical term for the injury is 'comminuted intra-articular tibial fracture'. I also suffered an acetabular cup fracture of the right hip - a serious derailment, in other words - and an open femoral intertrochanteric fracture in the same area. My spine was chipped in eight places. Four ribs were broken. My right collarbone held, but the flesh above it was stripped raw. The laceration in my scalp took 20 or 30 stitches. Yeah, on the whole, I'd say Bryan Smith was a tad conservative.

Mr Smith's driving behaviour in this case was eventually examined by a grand jury, who indicted him on two counts: driving to endanger (pretty serious) and aggravated assault (very serious, the kind of thing that means jail time). After due consideration, the District Attorney responsible for prosecuting such cases in my little corner of the world allowed Smith to plead out to the lesser charge of driving to endanger. He received six months of county jail time (sentence suspended) and a year's suspension of his privilege to drive. He was also put on probation for a year with restrictions on other motor vehicles, such as snowmobiles and ATVs. It is conceivable that Bryan Smith could be legally back on the road in the fall or winter of 2001.

David Brown put my leg back together in five marathon surgical procedures that left me thin, weak and nearly at the end of my endurance. They also left me with at least a fighting chance to walk again. A large steel and carbon-fibre apparatus called an external fixator was clamped to my leg. Eight large steel pegs called Schanz pins run through the fixator and into the bones above and below my knee. Five smaller steel rods radiate out from the knee. These look sort of like a child's drawing of sunrays. The knee itself was locked in place. I entered the hospital on 19 June. Around the 25th, I got up for the first time, staggering three steps to a commode, where I sat with my hospital johnny in my lap and my head down, trying not to weep and failing. You try to tell yourself that you've been lucky, most incredibly lucky, and usually that works because it's true. Sometimes it doesn't work, that's all. Then you cry.

A day or two after those initial steps, I started physical therapy. During my first session, I managed 10 steps in a downstairs corridor, lurching along with the help of a walker. One other patient was learning to walk again at the same time, a wispy 80-year-old woman named Alice who was recovering from a stroke. We cheered each other on when we had enough breath to do so. On our third day in the downstairs hall I told Alice, 'Your ass is showing, sonnyboy,' she wheezed, and kept going.

I came home to Bangor on 9 July, after a hospital stay of three weeks. I began a daily rehab program which includes stretching, bending, and crutch-walking. I tried to keep my courage and my spirits up. On 4 August, I went back to CMMC for another operation. When I woke up this time, the Schanz pins in my upper thigh were gone. I could bend my knee again. Dr Brown pronounced my recovery 'on course' and sent me home for more rehab and physical therapy. And in the midst of all this, something else happened. On 24 July, five weeks after Bryan Smith hit me with his Dodge van, I began to write again.

Stephen King's *Misery*

Reading *Misery*   Group work

So far you have explored the similarities between fiction and non-fiction writing. But what about the differences? Is the only difference that one is made up and the other is about real-life? To help you investigate this further, read the following extract from the beginning of Stephen King's novel *Misery*.

■   Read the extract from *Misery* aloud in your group.

■   Talk about your first responses to this as a piece of writing.

■   Draw up a list of statements comparing the two pieces. You should think about both the similiarities and the differences. You could use the sentence starters suggested here to help you.

'The Accident' is......, whereas *Misery* ....
Both 'The Accident' and *Misery*..... reveal....
In *Misery* Stephen King.... However, in 'The Accident'

Misery

1

umber whunnnn
yerrrnnn umber whunnnn
fayunnnn
These sounds even in the haze.

2

But sometimes the sounds – like the pain – faded, and then there was only the haze. He remembered darkness: solid darkness had come before the haze. Did that mean he was making progress? Let there be light (even of the hazy variety), and the light was good, and so on and so on? Had those sounds existed in the darkness? He didn't know the answers to any of these questions. Did it make sense to answer them? He didn't know the answer to that one either.

The pain was somewhere below the sounds. The pain was east of the sun and south of his ears. That was all he *did* know.

For some length of time that seemed very long (and so *was*, since the pain and the stormy haze were the only two things which existed) those sounds were the only outer reality. He had no idea who he was or where he was and cared to know neither. He wished he was dead, but through the pain-soaked haze that filled his mind like a summer storm-cloud, he did not know that he wished it.

Literary non-fiction

As time passed, he became aware that there were periods of nonpain, and these had a cyclic quality. And for the first time since emerging from the total blackness which had prologued the haze, he had a thought which existed apart from whatever his current situation was. This thought was of a broken-off piling which had jutted from the sand at Revere beach. His mother and father had taken him to Revere Beach often when he was a kid, and he had always insisted that they spread their blanket where he could keep an eye on that piling, which looked to him like the single jutting fang of a buried monster. He liked to sit and watch the water come up until it covered the piling. Then, hours later, after the sandwiches and potato salad has been eaten, after the last few drops of Kool-Aid had been coaxed from his father's big Thermos, just before his mother said it was time to pack up and start home, the top of the rotted piling would begin to show again – just a peek and flash between the incoming waves at first, then more and more. By the time their trash was stashed in the big drum with KEEP YOUR BEACH CLEAN stencilled on the side, Paulie's Beach Boys picked up

(*that's my name Paulie I'm Paulie and tonight ma'll put Johnson's baby oil on my sunburn* he thought inside the thunderhead where he now lived)

and the blanket folded again, the piling had almost wholly reappeared, its blackish, slime smoothed sides surrounded by sudsy scuds of foam. It was the tide, his father had tried to explain, but he had always known it was the piling. The tide came and went; the piling stayed. It was just that sometimes you couldn't see it. Without the piling, there *was* no tide.

This memory circled and circled, maddening, like a sluggish fly. He groped for whatever it might mean, but for a long time the sounds interrupted.

fayunnnn

red everrrrythinggg

umberrrr whunnnn

Sometimes the sounds stopped. Sometimes he stopped.

His first really clear memory of this now, the now outside the storm-haze, was of stopping, of being suddenly aware he just couldn't pull another breath, and that was all right, that was good, that was just peachy-keen; he could take a certain level of pain but enough was enough and he was glad to be getting out of the game …

''Breathe, goddam you!' the unseen voice shrieked, and he thought *I will, anything, please just don't do that anymore, don't infect me anymore,* and he *tried*, but before he could really get started her lips were clamped over his again, lips as dry and dead as strips of salted leather.

When she took her lips away this time he did not let her breath out but *pushed* it and whooped in a gigantic breath of his own. Shoved it out. Waited for his unseen chest to go up again on its own, as it had been doing his whole life without any help from him. When it didn't, he gave another giant whooping gasp, and then he was breathing again on his own, and doing it as fast as he could to flush the smell and taste of her out of him.

Normal air had never tasted so fine.

He began to fade back into the haze again, but before the dimming world was gone entirely, he heard the woman's voice muter: 'Whew! That was a close one!'

Not close enough, he thought, and fell asleep.

He dreamed of the piling, so real he felt he could almost reach out and slide his palm over its green-black fissured curve.

When he came back to his former state of semiconsciousness, he was able to make the connection between the piling and his current situation – it seemed to float into his hand. The pain wasn't tidal. That was the lesson of the dream which was really a memory. The pain only *appeared* to come and go. The pain was like the piling, sometimes covered and sometimes visible, but always there. When the pain wasn't harrying him through the deep stone grayness of his cloud, he was dumbly grateful, but he was no longer fooled – it was still there, waiting to return. And there was not just one piling but *two*; the pain was the pilings, and part of him knew for a long time before most of his mind had knowledge of knowing that the shattered pilings were his own shattered legs.

But it was still a long time before he was finally able to break the dried scum of saliva that had glued his lips together and croak out 'Where am I?' to the woman who sat by his bed with a book in her hands. The name of the man who had written the book was Paul Sheldon. He recognized it as his own with no surprise.

'Sidewinder, Colorado,' she said when he was finally able to ask the question. 'My name is Annie Wilkes. And I am –'

'I know,' he said. 'You're my number one fan.'

'Yes,' she said, smiling. 'That's just what I am.'

Your life as a story

This is your chance to put into practise what you have learned about the relationship between fiction and non-fiction writing.

- Think of something important, strange or perhaps frightening that happened to you recently. You will be writing about this incident in two different ways.

- First write a short non-fiction account of it (no more than a paragraph or two).

- Now write about the same incident again, but this time use it as the basis of a made-up story. Before you begin, think about the ways in which this version might be different. Forinstance, you do not need to tell the whole story, you could pretend it happened to someone else, you could describe the setting in more detail and so on.

- Practise reading your two versions out loud, ready for sharing with the rest of the class.

Fact or fiction?   Class work
- Take it in turns to read out extracts from your writing on the important or frightening incident. Talk about the similarities and differences between the two versions. Could you tell which was the fictionalised version? If so, how?

A final draft   Homework
- Write a final version of 'The Incident' using the features of both fiction and non-fiction writing in order to engage your reader.